ONE GIANT AWAY

TIMOTHY FLEMMING, JR.

ONE GIANT AWAY

TIMOTHY FLEMMING, JR.

T&J Publishers
A Small Independent Publisher
with a Big Voice

ISBN: 978-0-9962165-2-4

For more information, go to:
www.TimothyFlemmingJr.com
www.TandJPublishers.com
RevTFJr@gmail.com
BookCoach99@gmail.com
Facebook: Timothy Flemming, Jr.
Instagram: Timothy Flemming, Jr.

Other books by Timothy Flemming, Jr.:
Prophetic Patterns in the Bible (2010)
Exposing the Great Deception (2013)

To the one who has given us, His children, the power to conquer every giant, to speak to every mountain, to overcome every obstacle; the one who slew death over two-thousand years ago... just so that I could live today: Jesus the Christ. I am eternally grateful for the privilege just to be Yours.

Secondly, I would like to thank my wife, Jackie. You have been my backbone, my support, a friend, someone that God sent into my life to help make me the man I am today. Also, I dedicate this book to my kids: Timothy Flemming, III; Timera JaNae Flemming, and Jeremiah Flemming. May each of you grow-up to be fierce giant-killers in this world and live out the lives you were predestined by God to live.

Lastly, to all of my family, friends and supporters who have been right there with me from day one, sticking with me through all of my mistakes and shortcomings and never giving up on me; to those of you who continuously rooted me on and encouraged me to keep moving forward with my visions, goals and dreams, thank you.

"Nay, in all these things we are more than conquerors through him that loved us."—
Romans 8:37

TABLE OF CONTENTS

Introduction   11

Chapter 1: Desert Babies   15

Chapter 2: The Lion and the Bear   35

Chapter 3: From Whence Come Monsters   55

Chapter 4: Dominion   73

Chapter 5: Unconventional   93

Chapter 6: A Giant In My Stairway   111

Chapter 7: Talking Trash   125

Chapter 8: Did You Forget About
           The Other Ones?   145

INTRODUCTION

BEFORE WE JOURNEY TOGETHER down this delightful golden brick road of self-discovery, I want to answer one very important question: *Who is this book written for?*

First off, this book is for humans only—it is not necessary that sinless angels read this book. The contents of this book won't appeal to you if you have a sinless nature. This book is for normal human beings only. This is for those who forget to pray every now and then—or more often than what is expected. This book is for people who always "intend" to read their Bibles, but get too caught-up into watching television; too wrapped-up into checking their Facebook accounts, emails, and other things to stay focused like we would all like to do. This book is for those who said they would never lie again, fornicate again, smoke or drink again, look at another porn video, sink into another fit of depression; this book is for those who said they'd never be tempted by *that* (whatever *that* is), and then ended-up being tempted by *it*—and now feel like crap. This book is for the person who hates the very skin that they live in and often prays for change.

If that is you, then from one imperfect being to another, I'd like to formerly say, "Hello."

Welcome to the fight. Welcome to the war. Welcome to the battlefield that is called the Christian faith—you know, the one where both the best inside of you and the worst inside of you are quite often exposed. The unique thing about Christianity is it is the only faith that tells the truth about mankind: man is a dichotomy, a sweet-and-sour paradox walking around in flesh; man is sinful to the core; and yet, created in the image of a sinless God—this placing man in a precarious position where he must always recognize and choose between two natures.

I am sorry to be the bearer of bad news, but I must inform you of a very shocking—and terrifying—reality: you are not a robot. I know you were taught the opposite. In school, some teacher called you a highly advanced biological android that's programmed by Natural Selection to act and respond to certain stimuli within our material environment—in short, they said you're the product of evolution. But I'm here to tell you that you are much different than that. Actually, you possess something no Naturalist understands or knows about: a soul. You are very, very complex, containing natural and spiritual (or should I say immaterial, ethereal, hyper-physical) attributes and components. Science hasn't even begun to scratch the surface of the complexity of that organism that is called...mankind.

Although that would be an exciting conversation—discussing Creationism vs. Evolution—this book isn't written for that purpose; it is instead written for the purpose of encouraging you not to throw in the towel on yourself because you feel as if you have little to nothing to offer, or you feel as if you're too inadequate to be powerful, or you've been beaten down so much that you don't think you deserve to even be loved, accepted, or considered in life. I'm on a strict mission here to infiltrate the enemy's defenses (stronghold) which have been set-up around your mind, and to rescue your soul from the sadistic hands of despair. Some may say it's Mission Impossible, but God says all things are possible to them that believe—that means, I don't care how trapped you may think you are, how steeped in depression you may be, how far gone you may feel, how hopeless you may feel, how inadequate, useless, insignificant, messed-up, jacked-up, etc. you may feel, God can do wonders in and through you, but you have to give God a try and muster-up the intestinal fortitude to . . . believe.

Will you? Will you take a chance on God and believe Him? Will you take a chance and entertain a different set of thoughts than the ones you're probably used to and listen to what I'm about to tell you in this book? It's not like you have something to lose; you do, however, have everything to gain. You have before you the opportunity to gain the right perspective pertaining to your circumstances, the right view of yourself, the right understanding of God, the correct understanding of your past, an understanding of the power you possess through Christ to defeat every seemingly insurmountable odd sitting before you; you have the opportunity to gain the strength, confidence, and faith to be the giant killer you were created to be; to defeat the inner enemies of fear, timidity, low self-esteem, doubt, anxiety, and the negativity that drains you of your joy, zest, zeal, and anticipation of a greater tomorrow.

Will you believe with me today?

Lock arms with me. Get a song in your heart. Want to sing *I'm off to see the Savior, the wonderful Son of God*? Might as well because that's where we're headed.

CHAPTER 1

DESERT BABIES

"Even if my father and mother abandon me, the
LORD will hold me close."—Psalm 27:10
(New Living Translation)

ISOLATED, OVERLOOKED, AND ALONE, little David spent the majority of his childhood on the backside of a desert, far from the watchful eyes of his father, Yishai (Jesse). David's brothers reviled him as if he were an outcast, a blight on the family's name; his father viewed him as a mistake, a badge of shame hanging over his own head. David knew only scorn, shame, rejection, and pain growing up. This is, perhaps, the common denominator in the lives of all extraordinary men and women of faith: pain and rejection; misunderstandings and low expectations. And this is most hurtful when it comes from family.

As has been pointed out by sources, little David was often assigned to the backside of the desert by his own father and brothers where the most dangerous animals were known to roam—this placed him in jeopardy of becoming a victim of an animal attack. Basically, David's own father and brothers couldn't have cared less if he would have been killed while tending to the sheep; they deliberately placed him in harm's way. Not only did they not expect him to be anything in life, but they apparently wished he would have never been born. This is interesting when considering Jesse's role in the community. According to Jewish sources, Jesse was a member of the Sanhedrin, which was the religious authority in the land. So, how could a religious leader not care about the well-being of his own child? Or better yet, what thoughts might have passed through David's mind when considering the fact that his own father, who was a devoutly religious and well respected pillar of the community hailing from a distinguished household, practiced godliness in public but godlessness in private? *You thought you had family problems?*

There are several theories available as to why David was the object of contempt within his household. One theory comes from the Talmud, which is the only source that mentions the name of David's mother. According to the Talmud, David's father, Jesse, held a suspicion that his wife, Nitzevet, cheated on him and conceived David. To Jesse, David was the result of adultery. (*Have you ever been told that you were the byproduct of a mistake? David was.*) Although Nitzevet was innocent of the charges and

David really wasn't a result of adultery—Jesse, who was actually the one attempting to commit adultery by seeking to sleep with one of his handmaidens, instead ended up sleeping with his wife after she veiled herself the same way Leah, Jacob's wife did in order to trick him into sleeping with her; a scheme Nitzevet concocted after discovering her husband's adulterous plan—she remained under a cloud of suspicion throughout the duration of her life. She could relate to David, but was powerless to help him. She could only pray for retribution and healing, and ask God to bottle-up every tear that fell from her little David's eyes, and, perhaps, compensate him for his undeserved suffering; and that's just what God did.

Again, this is only one theory. Another theory claims that David's mother did commit adultery, and David resulted out of this affair. Truthfully, no one knows what happened. But whatever the case is, we are certain of one thing: according to the Bible, David was ill-treated by his brothers, and had been looked down upon by his own father—*oh, and we're all born with the sin nature, compliments of Adam.*

David had every reason to be hateful, bitter, and acrimonious in life, but he wasn't. By everyone's standards, David should have been an angry young man drowning in a pool of addiction and sneering at life while it passed him by, singing 'Who done me wrong' while licking his wounds and throwing himself a pity party. David could have easily become just another statistic; a boy who allowed the pain of his past to completely swallow the brightness of his future. David even experienced the modern version of what we call "church hurt" due to his own father, the religious leader in the community, being abusive towards him behind closed doors. David experienced an upbringing that could've easily caused him to be angry towards God due to feeling neglected and unjustly treated; he could have simply given up on life, love, happiness, goodness . . . and God; and I'm sure he thought about doing so. I'm sure David contemplated throwing away hope; I'm sure he pondered over and over in his mind the many reasons why he should have allowed hatred to grip his heart; but, for some reason, he didn't become hateful and bitter. Rather than lament his broken relationships with his father and brothers, David developed an entirely new family out of the scorpions, snakes and sheep in the desert; his sheep became his family. I can picture David naming each sheep: Simchu, Baruch, Samuel; Simchu, the newest addition to the flock, holding a special place in his heart. David would gladly die for any one of his sheep—and in time, he would be given multiple opportunities to prove such a devotion.

YOUR 'FAV FIVE'...OR SIX, OR SEVEN

One of the toughest things for people to deal with is rejection. No one likes it. It hurts...a lot. Oftentimes, rejection is viewed as a personal assault on one's significance and value. When someone turns us down, we feel as if they don't value us, see us as important, and see us as being good enough to be a part of their inner-circle or team. Other people's rejection of us has the tendency to make us examine and question ourselves, as if we're the ones with the problem. We don't always take into account the many factors that are the basic causes of rejection. For example, some people might reject you simply because they are too overbooked, too burned out, too distracted, or even too afraid to trust anyone else. It's not that you are the problem; it's just that their minds are somewhere else and you just happened to catch them at the wrong time. And there are some cases where people are fed wrong information concerning you, and this effects their decisions concerning you. Jealousy could be a factor: *they're jealous of you.* Fear could be a factor: *they are intimidated by you.* Arrogance could be a factor: *they think they're better than you.* But there's one factor many of us tend to forget about: spiritual compatibility. Some people just aren't meant to be a part of your life; God never intended for you to be in their inner-circle. Jesus, in John chapter 6, was rejected by over seventy of His disciples after they misinterpreted His words; however, those who were meant to stay—the original twelve—remained put. If Jesus had have taken it personally that the other seventy left Him, He would have overlooked His responsibility to the twelve world-shakers the Heavenly Father hand-picked and placed directly under His care (Luke 10:22; Matthew 10:1-2; John 6:70). It's a hard pill for some people to swallow—particularly, those who are arrogant enough to think they are irresistible, and that they don't deserve to be told "no" by anyone; people who believe they are entitled to get whatever they want when they want it—but everyone isn't assigned to us, and part of overcoming rejection is to understand this elementary truth and accept the fact that rejection doesn't necessarily mean you must change something about yourself or that you have a personality problem; it could be an indication that you're an eagle who's trying to make a home among the chickens. God protects us by letting the world reject us. In many cases, God is simply rerouting us to the right crowd that has been designated for us by allowing us to get turned down by the "desired crowd". The key is to make living to serve and please God our goal; and when we do this, God will guide our affairs and connect us with the right people (Proverbs 16:7).

The Heavenly Father brought the twelve disciples into Jesus' life. God brought Lydia into Paul's life (Acts 16:14). God sent Peter to Cornelius' home (Acts 10:25). God sent four hundred "mighty men" into David's life while he was in the wilderness running from the deranged, maniacal King Saul. Those who trust God, living according to His Word, tend to have their paths amazingly connected with others that serve to assist them in reaching their destinies as opposed to hindering them from reaching their destinies. This may even mean getting connected to a Judas—he did, after all, help Jesus get to the cross.

But without knowing God and His will for our lives, it is impossible for us to discern when God is shifting us to a place where "certain people" must fall off, and to the place where those who are assigned to us are waiting. It takes a special breed of people to help you fulfill God's task for your life. Anyone just won't due. And some folks are just plain toxic and bad for your spiritual health.

There are seasons when individuals you may have depended on for a long time will suddenly depart from your life—some for good reasons; some for your protection. There was a story told about a pilot who was flying a plane one day when several of the passengers noticed that there was a snake loose on the plane. They complained and panicked, but the pilot instructed them to sit down and fasten their seat belts. He then began to soar higher until the snake began flopping around and then died. The threat ended. One of the passengers asked the pilot, "What happened?" The pilot explained to them that snakes can't live at a certain altitude.

Growing up, one of my school teachers made a statement that sounded to me like another cheesy catch-phrase. She told us, "Your attitude determines your altitude." That was my teacher's attempt to motivate me and my peers to do right. To me, it was just another over-regurgitated, wildly rehearsed, fancy phrase used by people who love to sound deep. But today, I must say, I understand it now. I understand the significance of having the right attitude; however, today I also realize there is the tendency of many people to lean in the flawed direction of humanism when trying to motivate and inspire others. My teacher made a fatal mistake, one that's made by most of the world today: she assumed that a person can simply find it within themselves to be what God intended for them to be. She assumed that human nature has the ability to change its spots and stripes and climb above the pitfalls of the flesh. Her logic was backwards. Here's the Bible's version of that saying: Your altitude determines your attitude. While the world dumps tons of frustration on people by telling them that they must change their attitudes if they're going to succeed in life, and while we put pressure on our children and threaten them with the possibility of jail or homelessness if they don't reach within themselves and get a new perspective, God is saying it's not our attitudes that need to change but our altitudes that need to change. Make drawing closer to God the primary objective, not transforming yourself. We must earnestly seek God. When we fellowship with God, it becomes His responsibility to change us. The first thing that God will change is our understanding of who we are; and secondly, He teaches us new habits, which leads to new lifestyles and behaviors. The Bible says in Romans 12:1-3,

> "And so, dear brothers and sisters, I plead with you to give your bodies to God because of all he has done for you. Let them be a liv-

ing and holy sacrifice—the kind he will find acceptable. This is truly the way to worship him. **Don't copy the behavior and customs of this world, but let God transform you into a new person by changing the way you think.** Then you will learn to know God's will for you, which is good and pleasing and perfect. Because of the privilege and authority God has given me, I give each of you this warning: Don't think you are better than you really are. Be honest in your evaluation of yourselves, measuring yourselves by the faith God has given us." (NLT)

The biblical teaching is that we are to be transformed by God, not ourselves; and God, when transforming us, does so by changing the way we think using His Word. The world tries to train God out of us using evolution, atheistic worldviews masked as scientific thinking (true science is compatible with the Bible), and humanism (making us look within rather than look up to God), but God is the only individual who can change hearts, the only one who can change societies, the only individual that can heal the nations. We must learn to turn to Him. This is what made David unique and earned him the title "A man after God's own heart": David, despite all of his imperfections, knew the secret to defeating his own flesh and overcoming every obstacle set before him: seek after God and live a repentant life ("repentance" means "a change of thought that leads to a change of action").

Paul further reveals to us that as we draw closer to God, not only does He change our thoughts, but He reveals to us His will for us—our purposes and destinies: reasons for existing. A person who doesn't know who they are will be susceptible to the lies of Satan concerning them: that they're useless, they're no good, irredeemable, destined to follow the failures of their parents and ancestors, destined to die in their addictions, unable to overcome the challenges they're facing; that they'll always be a basket-case, a drug addict, an alcoholic, a pervert, a low-life, they will always be on welfare, they're bound to enter in and out of the revolving doors of the prison system, they're inferior to another person, they're less than someone else, they're a victim, etc. And here's the biggest lie: they weren't created with a purpose by a living and loving God; but instead, they're the product of a cosmic coincidence called The Big Bang and they just so happened to evolve from apes into humans over millions of years. And we wonder why many people act like animals, graveling over money, status, material things, and committing murder, deceiving, lying, swindling, and doing all manner of evil to others just to get ahead in life. Tell them they are animals and they'll act like animals. God knows the value of us knowing who we really are. When we discover our purposes in life, we'll find a motivation that can't come from anyone or anything besides the truth of God's Word. We'll arise from our graves of despair and move forward in the light of assurance with a level of confidence never before seen.

Being that I am a King's kid who is endowed by God with a purpose that's much bigger than me, money couldn't appeal to me, telling me that I would miss out on big cars and big mansions if I didn't get my lesson wasn't appealing to me either, nor did attempting to frighten me with prison and/or homelessness motivate me. I, like all of us were designed to be, am hardwired to unconsciously gravitate like a moth to a flame towards my purpose in life—that's a natural curiosity we're born with and would cultivate in life if not for the impositions of others, most of whom have lost their ability to dream. I was motivated by purpose, by my very reason for existing. I believed then and still believe now that knowing my purpose and fulfilling it is the ultimate satisfaction. When you're destined by God for greatness, there's an itch the world cannot scratch, and there's nothing the world can give you that can satisfy you; material things can't satisfy the hunger on the inside of you, a hunger for a higher purpose. You can't fill the void in your soul with material possessions and be satisfied. God never intended for stuff to take His place. Some people can't handle your quest for purpose; they're uncomfortable with your thirst for things that are invisible and immaterial; they get spooked by these aspirations and desires because they aren't controllable by others. People close to you probably call you strange, weird, and out of touch because your goals are different from theirs. When you finally begin to climb higher, they will start flopping around on the ground...and will eventually become dead weight in your life. Don't feel bad. Don't be disappointed. You should feel grateful that they were exposed. Anyone that can't ascend to the level God is taking you is not cut-out for you.

For all of you humanists out there, the Apostle Paul gave this warning: don't think of yourselves more highly than you should; but rather, view yourselves honestly and through the lens of God's Word. In other words, Paul was directly attacking the view that human nature is capable of changing itself, and that we're capable of transforming our world for the better outside of genuine repentance. For example, regarding the violence in our public schools today, reports reveal to us: before the 1960's (before prayer and the Bible were removed from schools), the main disciplinary problems teachers had out of students was chewing gum, violating the dress code, running in the halls, and talking out of term, but after prayer and the Bible were removed from all public schools in the 1960's the main disciplinary problems became assault, rape, gang activity, weapon possessions, and also assaults on teachers. Today, school shootings are rampant. Morality has almost disappeared. This is what happens when we replace biblical absolutes with moral relativism: we grow even more confused and dependent upon a vacillating human nature.

THE ART OF GETTING HIGH

There is a place where *snakes* can't survive—where demons can't dwell, deceivers can't deceive, anxiety disintegrates, fear is too afraid to venture, and where carnality melts away like butter in a hot oven: it's the secret place talked about by David in the 91st Psalm. There, David wrote, "He that dwelleth in the secret place of the Most High shall abide under the shadow of the Almighty" (vs. 1). David calls the presence of the Lord "the secret place". By "secret," David was explaining that the presence of the Lord—or should I say, the path leading to the presence of the Lord—is undiscovered and hidden from the carnal minded. Few know where this path lies. Few know where to look. All men secretly long to commune with God, but few know how. God cannot be accessed through drugs, the occult, philosophical or material means. This "path" is made known only to those who have a relationship with the Holy Spirit. God doesn't dwell in manmade traditions nor rest in the spotlight, and He doesn't dwell among the crowd. The "world" can never know the Holy Spirit (John 14:16-17). In Matthew 7:13-14, Jesus described the secrecy of God:

> "You can enter God's Kingdom only through the narrow gate. The highway to hell is broad, and its gate is wide for the many who choose that way. But the gateway to life is very narrow and the road is difficult, and only a few ever find it." (NLT)

Aside from the fact that the world, without the Holy Spirit's guidance, can't find this "path" of salvation (1 Corinthians 12:3; John 14:17), those who've packed into the arena of Christendom but haven't embraced the responsibilities of the faith (2 Timothy 3:5; Revelation 3:16) are equally as confused as the lost, not knowing the joys of God's holy presence; they have chosen religion over relationship and know nothing about the presence and anointing of God.

The Holy Spirit is the only one who can guide us into the Lord's presence. The Holy Spirit is the individual who urges us to pray, render praise to God, and seek His face. God calls us to a place of intimacy with Him in prayer because He's trying to lift us out of the reach of the devil and his minions. God is now trying to elevate us to a place in Him where anxiety perishes, where we develop a confidence that is impossible to drum-up in our flesh. God's presence is a place of safety, and it is also a place of preparation. When fellowshipping with God, He gives us peace, assurance that He is taking care of us, direction, and He overshadows us with His love.

If you are wondering how David was able to avoid becoming a basket-case in the midst of all he went through, let me tell you how: it was not that he was so special that he was above reproach, it was not that he was sinless (not by the least), it was not that he had something special "inside" of him that made him exceptional; the only reason David survived in that desert is because he was skilled at entering into the secret place of God's presence through worship. He was a skilled psalmist who wrote beautiful love poetry to God while in worship. David would sing to the Lord; he would dance before the Lord without a care or concern of who was looking; he would play musical instruments to the Lord while in worship; he would talk to the Lord all day and all night. David is the same person who gave us the remedy for dealing with an afflicted soul. He said we must meditate on God's Word "day and night" (Psalm 1:2)—"meditate" in the Hebrew means "utter; speak out loud." David said we must "sing unto the Lord a new song" (Psalm 96:1), which implies be creative in our worship of the Lord. He said we must keep God's praises on our lips and in our mouths "at all times" (Psalm 34:1)—talk about God more than you do your problems. This all takes practice. It takes practice to even beat your flesh into submission and spend time with God before starting your day. Your flesh tells you to worry; the Holy Spirit whispers to you, "Hey, come and follow Me. I'm taking you to see the Father, the Creator of heaven and earth, the King. He's waiting for you in an undisclosed location. Just follow Me." It becomes apparently clear what David meant when he wrote, "Even if my father and mother abandon me, the Lord will hold me close." He lived it! David, being that he was abandoned by his father and knew his mother was powerless to help him, found God's presence to be an escape and the Heavenly Father to be a father figure to him. He discovered that God is always close to us when we feel abandoned, disappointed, rejected, unwanted, and worthless. Our issue isn't that God isn't near; it's that we hardly seek to draw closer to Him. We enjoy our pity parties and don't want to soar higher into the presence of God. That's a costly mistake that sets us up for failure; and sets us up to become the angry, acrimonious, bitter, hate-filled, disgruntled, discontent, despondent, depressed, mentally oppressed, stressed, irritable, anxious, fearful, unstable, unhappy, boorish, cankerous, and even unbearable potato heads we often are. We can cover up these emotions with "things", artificial happiness, temporary bliss, parties, clubbing, alcohol and drugs, sex, etc., but at the end of the day, we are still left with the underlying problem of an unfulfilled life, an empty existence, a troubled mind, a ton of regrets gnawing away at our sanity, a heap of fears sitting in our laps, and demonic oppression.

THE BLESSING OF ABANDONMENT

Every so often people will take off their masks and reveal their true selves. And don't snicker or judge—you're one of them. From time to time you and I will make promises we can't keep and let people down in life. We may miss an appointment, cancel a date, not come through with a promise, make a mistake, drop the ball (figuratively speaking), fail at a task, fail to plan for unforeseen events, plan inadequately, place ourselves in precarious positions, not catch

the plane home to be by someone's side in time, not
have the right words to say at times, not be the best
company at times—at times, we become all too...hu-
man; yes, human. It's simply a human trait to fall, to
fail, to mess-up, and disappoint. In fact, God placed
a spiritual law in existence that serves as a kind of
"mistake insurance"—it's called mercy. In Proverbs
28:13, God said if we "confess" our sins we "shall receive mercy," and in Mark 11:25 Jesus said only if we
forgive others will God forgive us—in other words,
the merciful shall receive mercy, and those who are
so cold and stern that they can't overlook the mistakes of others and be merciful will find themselves
in the position where they will need mercy but won't
find it. We're all sinful, accident prone, short-sight-
ed creatures—that's a human trait, the byproduct of
Adam's fall from grace in the Garden of Eden; and it
is in light of this revelation that forgiveness blooms,
that understanding develops, that unfair and unre-
alistic expectations are crushed, that imperfection is
embraced, and healing is administered; it is in light
of this revelation that God's grace is understood.

Here's an old saying: Sometimes God has to
knock us on our backs in order to get us to look up.
That's unfortunately accurate! We forget to look up
for looking around. We forget to talk to God for being so consumed with talking to those we physically
see. We all tend to lose sight of God while pursuing
after the things we want in life. But we should all be
relieved to know God is not easily hurt and offend-

ed; that God doesn't give up on us so easily. God has a way of bringing us back to our knees, causing us to turn back to Him when we stray, and getting our attention when we get too focused on other things. One of the things God does is sit back and allow us to have our hopes and dreams crushed by those we depend upon, allow us to taste sour disappointment from people, and allow us to get our hearts broken. God doesn't have to manipulate people into hurting us; all He has to do is let human nature be itself and do what it does best: be flawed and impotent.

David claimed that God is closest to us in our deepest pain. If everyone else writes you off, God is there (Psalm 34:18). Jesus doesn't just see your pain; He can relate to it through personal experience—for He, too, was rejected by His brothers and sisters; He, too, was misunderstood by men in his community; He, too, was accused of being the product of adultery; He, too, lived under a cloud of suspicion while His mother lived under a cloud of shame; He, too, was given the backside of the desert in life, and was viewed with scorn, contempt, and low expectations; men wrote Him off too, and cursed Him. Men may write you off and curse you to wonder out of sight, in the backside of the desert; they may curse you to seemingly meander eternally within the confines of isolation and shame, but their rejection is just one of the many tools used to make you...a king and a giant slayer.

CHAPTER 1 OBJECTIVES:

•Focus less on the people who reject you and more on the people who receive and celebrate you. Pour into the people who are there with you and show them appreciation.

•Don't perceive rejection as a personal attack against you; but rather, realize that rejection is a normal part of life and take it as a personal challenge to improve in important areas in your life.

•Stay away from the wrong crowds. Gently and kindly sever ties with those who keep you in sin and destructive behaviors. Do so by choosing not to participate in activities with them that are sinful, and by stating your position that your goal is to live the life that God has called you to live. Invite them to join you in pursuing God rather than following them in their pursuit of hell.

•Seek God to discover your purpose in life, and then ask God to send the right people around you to help you fulfill His purpose for your life.

•Ask God for the wisdom and discernment to know who He has assigned to your life. Also, ask God to help you be a blessing in the lives of others. Focus on serving others rather than yourself.

•Make a new habit: Spend several minutes every morning thanking and praising God. Get use to praising and thanking God. Make the choice to focus on the blessings of God in your life rather than focus so much on all of your disappointments.

ONE GIANT AWAY

CHAPTER 2

THE LION AND THE BEAR

"Thy servant slew both the lion and the bear: and
this uncircumcised Philistine shall be as one of them,
seeing he hath defied the armies of the living God."—
1 Samuel 17:36

I T TAKES COURAGE TO WALK BY FAITH. I mean, as a person, if you don't have any guts, Christianity will teach you to have some. God will toss you into the deep water and teach you how to trust Him. He will put you in a position where you only have two options: trust Him or drown. Either you're going to make the willing—and might I add, daring—decision to believe God and cling onto the belief that He will take care of you—even if things don't turn out the way you want them to, believe that God has a bigger plan in the situation—or you will perish in the waters of strife, confusion, depression, anxiety, and bitterness. Faith will preserve your health and sanity and teach you to relinquish control and relax; doubting God will cause your health to diminish by coaxing you into believing that you are omnipotent and omnipresent, by causing you to attempt to control and micromanage every single situation, and by keeping you uptight and full of stress, tension, and worry. So, which one will it be: faith or doubt?

It takes courage to trust God, but God knows we don't automatically know how to walk by faith; so, He teaches us how to walk by faith by introducing us to small challenges. But before we cover these challenges, let's look at the definition of courage.

Courage. What is it? It's defined as "the ability to do something that frightens one; strength in the face of pain and grief" (Webster). Courage isn't the absence of fear; it's the presence of a much deeper concern, one that propels us to press on in-spite of fear. If you don't believe that, then take the case of a woman named Lydia Angiyou. In 2006, in northern Quebec, while walking along the coast, a polar bear (an animal that weighs between 750 to 1,500lbs) came charging towards her seven year old son and his friends. What Lydia did next is something only love can drive someone to do: she positioned herself right in the middle of the bear and the children, offering herself as a human shield to give them an opportunity to escape. She was more concerned about the safety of her son and his friends than she was her own safety. Was she scared of the beast? Certainly! But what frightened her more than the beast's sharp claws and teeth was the thought of losing her son, and watching his friends get mauled to death. Lydia's case is just one of many examples of individuals who overcame fear by losing sight of themselves.

A brave man is really just a coward who's too afraid of losing that which he truly loves. David was afraid of losing his sheep. Joshua and Caleb were too afraid of losing God's favor to let a couple of giants dissuade them from obeying God. John revealed in Revelation 12:11 that the only way to defeat Satan in this world is to be more afraid of losing your soul than losing your life. Jesus explained that we should be more afraid of God than man because man can only afflict the body, but God can destroy both the body and the soul eternally in hell (Matthew 10:28). Even demons have enough sense to be afraid of God—actually, they are way more than afraid; they are terrified (James 2:19). The horror movies make demons seem invincible; they are even depicted in some instances as being more powerful than God; but in reality, God and His saints is the bogeyman to Satan and his demons. Hollywood got it backwards. Embrace your natural tendency to fear, but question what you fear.

You're not a loser just because you have fears. You're not wicked simply because you grow afraid to trust God and step out on faith at times. We all grow weak in the knees when God challenges us to step out on faith. I grew weak in my knees once during a Sunday morning service when the Holy Spirit challenged me to step out on faith and give a seed offering of over $1,800, which was all of the money I had in my bank account at the time. I immediately began rebuking Satan when the unction came upon me to sow that seed, even though I did sense that it wasn't the devil pushing me to make such a sacrifice. After a few minutes of wrestling with the Holy Spirit, I finally obeyed God even while being afraid to do so. I sowed that seed. And I didn't go back to my seat rejoicing either; I went back thinking about the court case that I had, the expenses I needed to pay, and all of the other things I needed and desired to do with that money. But I'll confess that getting blessed with $37,000 afterwards exceeded my expectations. Now, I'm afraid to not step out on faith and trust God in my giving, as well as in every other area of my life. I'm afraid of what I might be forfeiting by being disobedient when God instructs me to do something. Remember that every instruction from God carries a harvest. So, what harvests are you forfeiting? Look at tests of faith as opportunities to be blessed, not as inconveniences that come to disrupt your life. What life? You're already in need of a blessing! You could use a few "divine disruptions" right now anyway.

You aren't less than another person because your knees might buckle or you may tremble in the face of a big challenge. Don't let people fool you. The biggest fool, according to the Bible, is the man who doesn't operate in a healthy sense of fear. The healthy fear is what Scripture calls *the fear of God*. Solomon wrote, "The fear of the Lord is the beginning of wisdom" (Proverbs 9:10). He also wrote, "The fear of the Lord is to hate evil" (Proverbs 8:13). Being conscious of God—His presence; His watchful eyes; of the fact that He sees everything and that He will ultimately judge all men—is the number one behavior modifier in the world. Without this awareness, men commit tremendous evil. In fact, as David explained in Psalm 14:1, "Only fools say in their hearts, 'There is no God.' They are corrupt, and their actions are evil; not one of them does good!" (NLT). Basically, what David was saying is this: In order for people to commit evil deeds, they must first banish God from their minds; that way, they won't have a conscience and a sense of right and wrong to block them from doing what they desire to do. It's smart to be afraid of some things. Embrace God's mercy, but fear Him enough to work out your "own soul salvation with fear and trembling" (Philippians 2:12).

LOVE < FEAR

The Bible says, "Perfect love casts out fear" in 1 John 4:18. By "fear," the Apostle John is talking about the fear of anything and anyone besides God. Love will overpower our fear of what people might say, think, or even do to us when we're executing God's will.

So, God has you in a desert. It seems as if you can't get to that desired place in life. You're stuck with a bunch of bleating sheep. You wish you were in the palace right now, chillin' in a comfortable and luxurious lazy-boy, being fed grapes and finely prepared meats as if you are at a 5-star Brazilian restaurant. Right now, unfortunately, things aren't lining up the way you want. You pray, plant seed offerings, pray, plant, etc., but nothing seems to hoist you out of the place where you are; and then God places it on your heart to pick-up this book; and while reading it, you just happen to come across this revelation: *While you're waiting for the palace, God is trying to develop a deeper love in your heart for the sheep. He wants to develop in you the heart for the sheep that David possessed. Why? Because God isn't looking for kings to sit on the throne in the palace; He's looking for shepherds...who understand that the needs of His people are more important than the comforts of the flesh.* To a selfish person, the palace will only exasperate their selfishness and bring destruction; to a shepherd, the palace will provide more resources for them to use to accomplish God's will. What's your motivation: having your ego stroked or living out your purpose?

Dr. Martin Luther King, Jr. is known as one of the greatest civil rights champions in history—his deeds are solidified in history; his name is etched in the annuls of time. But while many people praise his strong stance for justice, they overlook his *shepherd mentality*. He wasn't great because he was a great orator; he was great because he was willing to sacrifice his life for justice and equality. He abandoned the comforts of luxury for the perils of adversity. Actually, Dr. King, Jr. went against the advice of many close to him after he decided to march against injustice. People close to him actually told him he was being a fool, he was unnecessarily putting his life in danger; but we celebrate Dr. King, Jr. today because he chose to love justice more than the comforts of luxury. He loved and feared the right things. Still, we must all recognize that there's something far greater at stake than racial reconciliation: people are falling into the eternal pits of hell in droves daily; so, who is going to prioritize winning souls above themselves?

God is trying to teach us to walk in His love. His desire is for others to be saved, and love is what accomplishes this goal. But what is the love of God? Is it the same mushy, gushy, touchy, feely thing that the world embraces? No! Far from it! This is what the Bible describes as the love of God: (1) Love is unconditional. It isn't something to be earned. God loves us in-spite of ourselves. (2) Love is not passive and accepting of sin because sin separates us from God and condemns us to eternal damnation. In Ezekiel 3:17-21, God spoke to His prophet and told him to speak and warn the Israelites of their sins; and if he failed to do so the people would perish in their sins, but God would hold him accountable for not warning them. In 1 Corinthians chapter 5, Paul explained that love entails not being passive and allowing sinful practices to persist in the house of God, even to the point of kicking those out who

41

insist on walking in deliberate disobedience to God for the sake of not corrupting the rest of the body (Believers). Hebrews 12:6 says those who God loves He chastises; therefore, God, as a loving Father, will never sit back and ignore the wrong that we do. He'll address our wrong and spank us when we get out of line. God shakes us when He has to, and He'll do whatever it takes to free us from the bondage of sin...because sin is what separates us from Him (Isaiah 59:2; John 9:31). God gives us commandments to protect us, not to stop us from having fun. "Fun" is when we can enjoy life the right way: the way that prevents diseases, confusion, strife, and other negative consequences. Paul said regarding love:

> "...love is patient and kind, is not jealous, boastful, proud, rude; doesn't demand its own way; isn't irritable, doesn't keep record of the wrong done; doesn't rejoice over injustice, but rejoices whenever the truth wins out; it never gives up, never loses faith, is always hopeful, and endures through every circumstance." (1 Corinthians 13:4-7, NLT)

Love isn't an emotion; it's a choice. You must choose to forgive and put another person's reconciliation to God before your own wants and desires. This is why Paul, in 2 Corinthians 5:11-21, said every Christian has been given a ministry: he called it the ministry of reconciliation. This is what it means to love someone else: desire that they be reconciled to God more than anything. Here's a good example of this: If a man truly loves a woman, he'll sacrifice his own hormones and sexual desires just to ensure that her soul doesn't fall into jeopardy, keeping in mind that fornication will satisfy the flesh temporarily but will also damn the soul eternally; in other words, he will choose to marry her or leave her alone rather than lead her into sin due to selfishness—and vice-versa. When Jesus asked Peter if he loved Him, He implied to Peter that the way he would demonstrate his love for God was by feeding God's sheep—by "feeding," Jesus meant nourishing and training people in the Word of God; and nourishing and training others in the Word of God consists of more than just talking about the Word, it also consists of living according to God's Word before people. Paul wrote in Romans chapter 14, "For we don't live for ourselves or die for ourselves . . . So let's stop condemning each other. Decide instead to live in such a way that you will not cause another believer to stumble and fall" (vs. 7, 13; NLT).

Many people assume that you have to get out and save the world after you become a Christian; but in reality, you don't start with the world, you start with those closest to you. Try to reconcile your family members to Christ; work on friends and work associates. Do you have a nephew or niece who could use some guidance? In the book of 1 Peter chapter 3, Peter instructed wives to lead their unbelieving husbands to Christ through their lifestyles and respect-ful attitudes. In 1 Timothy 5:8, Paul tells fathers to live the faith by focusing on their family's needs and not neglecting them. Many opportunities for minis-try can be found in your home, community, job, etc.

THE BEASTS BEFORE THE MONSTER

David's love for his sheep mirrored God's love for His sheep (the church). God saw that David's heart was in the right place and rewarded him. Interest-ingly enough, God did the same thing for David's son, Solomon, who, instead of asking God for mon-ey, asked God for wisdom to "lead God's people". As a result of desiring to serve God's people above ev-erything else, God gave Solomon unparalleled wis-dom and riches. David was learning a crucial lesson during those days in the desert, one that would set the model for the rest of his life. He would spend the rest of his life living to serve the people of God, meeting their needs all while making sure they were protected not only from the physical enemies of the land, but also the idolatrous practices around them. David gained this protective instinct in the desert where he fought to spare his sheep from the mouths of a lion and a bear. His love for his sheep greatly surpassed his fear of death, and caused him as a little child to do the extraordinary: face creatures much bigger than himself. This wasn't a coincidence. God was watching over David and protecting him, and it was due to God's protection that David was able to succeed against those beasts. David learned through these experiences that when a person is busy being about the Father's business, God will place a hedge of protection around them and shield them from things that would ordinarily devour them. David's extraordinary confidence in the provisions and protection of God started in the desert. God trains us to walk by faith in the desert—in the small things first. Faith is perfected in stages—by taking baby steps. If you can't trust God to pay a $700 rent, how can you trust God to finance a multi-million dollar business venture? If you can't tithe today due to fear, how will you operate in the faith tomorrow to give millions to the Kingdom? Jesus said we must prove ourselves to be faithful with little before God blesses us with much (Luke 16:10). We must learn to face the lions and bears in our lives before we dare talk about taking on the monsters waiting for us up ahead. Your lion may be your tongue—tame it! Your bear might be your job—learn how to get there on time and be respectful to those in authority. Master forgiveness before taunting the monster of marriage. Little obstacles in your life are faith exercises meant to teach you how to trust God. The little areas the Holy Spirit is convicting you in—areas of integrity, honesty, and discipline—determine whether or not God will be able to lead you into the "Promised Land" where the giants are waiting. It was a small thing called doubt that caused the Israelites to lose their opportunity to enter into the Promised Land under Moses. It was a little thing called a temper that caused Moses to lose his opportunity to enter into the Promised Land. Practice mastering your temper, budgeting, tithing, prioritizing, thanking God for what He has already given you rather than complaining about what you don't have and where you are in life, not complaining about everything that's not going right for you, not always saying what's on your mind (Proverbs 29:11 tells us only a fool speaks their whole mind), saying "no," not being overly critical of others, not harboring grudges, not sweating the small stuff, not neglecting to spend time with God daily, appreciating those God has placed in your life, and not neglecting to read God's Word. Practice applying the Word of God to your life in everyday situations. Practice doing what God says to do in His Word—for, when we do this, we demonstrate to God that we're able to handle the bigger blessings, which come with bigger challenges. New levels mean new devils.

IN THE JAWS OF DISCOURAGEMENT

If faith breeds encouragement, then doubt breeds discouragement. If courage is a prerequisite of walking by faith, then the loss of courage is a prerequisite of walking in doubt. Discouragement is perhaps Satan's favorite weapon. He knows that a person who is discouraged by a lack of results will stop praying; and if they stop praying, how can they expect to get results. Discouragement puts us in a vicious cycle of apathy and defeat. If we pray and ask God to bless us with something and we don't get it, we tend to get discouraged and avoid asking for other things; and as soon as we cut God off, we'll turn to other things and methods of obtaining our goals, and that's when demonic spirits come and coax us further into sin.

I can recall many times being angry with God and being discouraged. I waived my fists at the sky quite a few times; and even worse than waiving my fists, I just didn't even bother acknowledging God in the course of my day many days due to disappointment. The biggest incident that brought discouragement my way was when I witnessed the passing of my oldest brother in October of 1993. Before then, I was super confident in prayer. I believed I had the ability to pray anything away that I didn't want in my life. I thought prayer was a tool used to control God. Boy, was I wrong! My oldest brother was on his way to church—he was a minister who had just finished preparing his message for Sunday morning. It was sunny out; nothing out of the ordinary. But that day was etched in my memory because that was the day that my brother, a 22 year old young man with what appeared to be a bright future ahead of him, was hit and killed by a drunk driver. The driver of the van hit my brother's Honda and knocked it into a ditch. My mother and I were the first ones to arrive on the scene immediately following the accident. Panic gripped my mother's heart, but I attempted to drum up all of the faith that I had on the inside of me and believe God for a supernatural healing. The ambulance came and pulled my brother's body out of the twisted metal of the wreckage—he was still alive at the time, although unconscious. They then rushed him to the hospital. While my mother and I trailed behind the ambulance I convinced myself that God was going to heal my brother and that this nightmare would simply turn into a testimony of God's healing grace...but that didn't happen. No matter how much I prayed and believed God for a healing, my brother passed away that day due to internal bleeding. I was devastated that he died, but even more crushed that my prays didn't change his fate. At that moment, my gripe became with God. The signs clearly pointed to God's hand being involved even before the accident. God was subtly setting our family up for the tragedy to come, but it was still difficult to embrace the idea that my prayers couldn't stop death in that situation. Behind this ordeal, discouragement set it.

Unanswered prayer leads to frustration. Frustration is what I call a subtle disease of the mind. It starts like a cancer, like an afterthought in the back of the mind; it then grows with time, feeding on the disappointments that keep mounting up; and then, like a raging wildfire, it spreads throughout the soul; like a cancer, it spreads through every limb and eats away at us until one day, without fully knowing why, we've become nearly unrecognizable and seemingly beyond saving; that's when discouragement sets in.

What is discouragement? It's "a loss of confidence or enthusiasm; dispiritedness." A loss of confidence (*a firm trust in someone or something*) and enthusiasm (*intense and eager enjoyment, interest or approval*) describes many people today, both in and out of church. So many people have simmered in frustration until that frustration became discouragement, and they've suddenly lost their excitement in life over the things of God and over the promises of God. Some have stopped believing the words that declared by God's ministers, and they no longer believe miracles are real, deliverance from addictions is possible, and healing from diseases and sicknesses is possible. They've stopped believing! They now say to themselves, *Why hype yourself up to believe in the power of prayer and to expect changes when change is not going to come? Why even do that to yourself? That's self-inflicted torture! It's better to simply let nature take its course rather than look for miracles (God's bending of the rules of nature), isn't it?* The Israelites experienced this type of frustration when, after being in slavery for over four hundred years and receiving no answer to their prayers for deliverance from their bondage, they finally gave up on the hope of being delivered. The Bible says, "Moses told the people of Israel what the LORD had said, but they refused to listen anymore. They had become too discouraged by the brutality of their slavery" (Exodus 6:9; New Living Translation).

It's easier to not believe in miracles, not hope for changes, not anticipate a blessing, not live with expectations of a move of God and not put any stock into the promises made in God's Word than it is to believe. It's easier to get lost in the bland routine of church activities and regress into a state of religion and tradition than it is to expect an explosive visitation of God's supernatural presence in our lives. If we have waited for something for a certain period of time and it didn't come right away, we usually give up on it and write it off...and then make adjustments to go on without it. Some people have written God off: they've written His promises off; they've written His power off; and the only thing they're holding on to is an empty shell of religious routines and traditions that somehow satiate their appetite for fleshly gratification—in other words, self-righteousness keeps them feeling pious. Their desire to appear pious is fueled by their desire to be accepted by their neighbors, not God. *God?* They barely believe in Him, or they've taken the position of agnostics and declared Him to be too indifferent to be concerned about our earthly affairs: so, although God exists, He's not really involved with nor responsible for anything that goes on in our lives—that's solely our responsibility. That's not true! But some people have convinced themselves that by not "pestering" God with their personal problems they are actually doing Him a favor. They tell themselves, "He is too preoccupied with things above to be bothered with my petty problems. So, I'll take some of the load off of Him and handle my own issues. He'll thank me for it later." They are not helping God; they're actually depriving Him of something He greatly desires: the chance to show His power (2 Chronicles 16:9).

God understands our frustrations. He really does. The Bible declares that our High Priest, Jesus the Christ, knows and has experienced the feelings of our infirmities (weaknesses) (Hebrews 4:15). Jesus experienced the anguish of despair and the sense of frustration while dwelling among us; He even experienced the pain of unanswered prayer. *God in the flesh dwelling among men, not having His prayers answered? That sounds preposterous, doesn't it?* Yes! It is difficult to believe...and yet, it happened! While in the Garden of Gethsemane, Jesus actually prayed a prayer that was rejected by the Father. Whoever said just because you want something God has to give it to you? Even God rejected a request that *He* offered up that was contrary to His divine will and plan.

What I didn't understand when I was younger was that prayer isn't for the purpose of controlling God; but rather, it's for the purpose of ensuring that we stay aligned with God. God is leading this dance, not us; and we must make sure we follow His lead... even if it takes us someplace we're not excited about going. It later dawned on me on that day: God prevented me from being involved in that accident with my brother when a situation arose that caused me to have to get out of the car the moment before the accident—yes, I was in the car with him just moments before the accident, and would have been killed also had God not intervened at the last minute. I recalled how God prompted my brother to call my dad out of the blue just before he got on the road just so they could have the opportunity to talk one last time. I recalled several strange events leading up to the accident: for example, my dad, who was out of town at the time at a Benny Hinn crusade, had just been prayed for and prophesied to before the accident by Evangelist Hinn that he was going to need a double touch of God's anointing because of something that was getting ready to happen; and later that day, after returning from the crusade, the hotel mysteriously kicked him out of his room for no reason, thereby forcing him to get on the road and head back home around the time of the accident. Basically, God was preparing everyone for the tragedy. He already knew what was to come. This was something that was set in His purpose. We get angry because, to be honest, God doesn't do what we want Him to do; He won't allow Himself to be controlled by us. But real faith is about trusting God, not controlling Him; and once I accepted this, I discovered that when God moves, He is thinking a million steps ahead of us. We don't see how even a tragedy can shape up to be a blessing in our lives down the road. We want to hold on to people, not knowing that God has greater plans. And it's important to remember that death for a Believer is the one thing that frees us and allows us to be eternally joined to the Father in heaven. When a Christian dies, they finally go home—free from pain and suffering. But selfishness blinds us to this truth.

I simply needed to stop being selfish and trust God. I had to learn that when Jesus made the statement while on earth that He does nothing unless the Father instructs Him to, He was revealing the secret to prayer: prayer is about listening to the Holy Spirit, praying what He tells us to pray, saying what He tells us to say and doing what He tells us to do. That's real faith. If the Holy Spirit tells you to rebuke the spirit of death off of someone, then rebuke it. If the Holy Spirit compels you to go and pray for a person who's sick or afflicted, then go and pray for them. God already has a plan in mind; He simply needs you to be the vehicle for Him to execute *His* will.

Misunderstanding creates selfishness, which begets wrong expectations, which begets frustration; and frustration tosses us into the mouth of discouragement; but a genuine faith built on the proper understanding of God's Word will cause us to grab discouragement by its mane and strike it right between the eyes with a death blow . . . and then return to a sense of urgency and excitement to pray just so that we can *hear* and *follow* God. You'll be confident not in your ability or might, but in the ability and might of God, resting assured in Him. If He tells you to kill Goliath, you will then go in the power of His might, and there will be no second guessing whether or not you will be victorious. This is God's way of teaching us how to trust Him and follow His lead . . . because trusting Him and following His instructions down to every detail is the only way we can kill...monsters.

53

CHAPTER 2 OBJECTIVES:

•Pray and ask God to fill your heart with His love.

•Look up all of the Bible verses about God's love that you can find and begin to study them.

•Practice making the spiritual well-being of others priority above your fleshly wants and desires.

•Make a list of the internal challenges that you face and the bad habits you currently possess—procrastination, a temper, your tongue, anger, communication skills, etc.—and then work on them. A great way to gain mastery over these things is to devote time to studying them through books. Another method of dealing with these things is to seek out counseling. But in either case, you can't deal with a problem you don't know exist or are unwilling to acknowledge. Remember: Don't allow your gifts to take you where your character can't keep you.

•Ask God to perform a supernatural miracle in your life today. Whether it be a healing, a financial miracle, or deliverance from an addiction, whatever it is, ask God to perform it and believe that He is going to perform it today. The purpose of this exercise is to activate a higher level of faith by being daring enough to ask God to demonstrate His supernatural power. Don't be handicapped and imprisoned by reason and carnal understanding—the realm of miracles operates outside of reason, logic and carnal understanding. That's why they're called miracles. Challenge yourself to believe in miracles today.

CHAPTER 3

FROM WHENCE COME MONSTERS

"We even saw giants there, the descendants of Anak..."—Numbers 13:33 (NLT)

M Y EYES WERE HEAVY AND MY BODY TIRED; my mind weary of the trouble that drove me each night out of the bed to roam the halls of my parents' home. I felt as if I were the walking dead; and perhaps, looked the part. I hadn't slept in days. I hadn't eaten in days. I couldn't concentrate in school. I was twelve years old and was living in a private hell.

For months this had been going on. The visions were getting worse with time. *They* were everywhere: spiders. They were on the walls, the floors, in my bed at night, in my food, in the backseat of my parents' cars, under the desks at school, under the toilet seats—they were everywhere! Hallucinations? Maybe. Visions? Perhaps. Whatever the case was, it was torture! It was torment! It was unbearable! My mom took me to see a psychiatrist; and once there, I was asked a bunch of questions and placed on medication. The solutions I was given were simple: *think about something good; picture yourself in a peaceful place; etc.* I found this to be useless advice. The visions continued, growing progressively worse; they got so bad that I was admitted into a hospital. Night after night I walked the halls of that hospital, staring into the ceiling lights above, unable to sleep. While in that center, I met many other kids who were experiencing troubles, though none were as intense as mine. Being the youngest and the only Black kid in the program, I saw a lot: kids who came from affluent households but were hate-filled, kids who wrestled with serious drug-addictions despite coming from good households, kids who resented their parents although they had more *stuff* than they could ever want, highly promiscuous teenage girls, and even one suicide-obsessed teenage boy with a charming personality and dashing good looks that captivated all of the other girls—and even several of the adult nurses. Thinking back on it now, it amazes me how Satan has such a tight grip on today's youth. Despite having all of the money in the world, hopelessness and despair, suicide and anger, depression and demonic oppression is ravaging people from all socio-economic backgrounds and ethnicities. Many are trapped in the devil's cauldron, stuck in a web of spiritual deception, looking for deliverance.

My fate changed one Sunday morning when my mother picked me up and took me to a church to hear my oldest brother (the late Aric B. Flemming, Sr.) preach. He was the guest minister at a church that day. His message was right down my lane. The title of it was "When you're caught-up in a spider's web". I was touched by his words as he declared that Satan is cunning, and he'll trap us through sin; but when we find ourselves trapped in a "web of satanic bondage" we must learn to call on the name of Jesus and ask Him for deliverance. He also said something that stuck with me more than anything: he said we must learn to "plead the blood of Jesus"; for, it is His blood that gives us power over demonic spirits. That day, at twelve years old, I went home and practiced what I heard preached from that pulpit. I asked Jesus to come into my heart and save me, then I stated these words: "I plead the blood of Jesus over my mind and declare: Satan, you have no authority over me in Jesus name." That very moment a peace came over me and I felt a weight literally lifting off of my shoulders—I physically felt it lifting. That night was the first night I slept uninterrupted in months. The nightmares ceased instantly. I hadn't taken anymore medication and didn't need anymore counseling. I left that center. And from that day until now, I had not had a single episode. I received supernatural deliverance. That experience was my first real encounter with the supernatural realm.

THE MONSTER SQUAD

No one really discerned during my ordeal what was the root cause of the nightmares and visions I was having. It was assumed that there was a natural explanation behind what I was going through. What shifted my understanding was the reality that it was a spiritual action—the denunciation of demonic authority over my life—that brought deliverance. This led me later on in life to investigate what really happened to me as a child. Many of the answers I sought came while in Bible College. While there, I took a course entitled *Spiritual Warfare*, in which the revelation of demons and their activities was provided. I was shocked to discover that Jesus referred to demons as serpents and arachnids (scorpions). I also came across a reference to demons being described as locusts in Revelation chapter nine, and as frogs in Revelation chapter thirteen. Is it a coincidence that what I struggled with were visions of arachnids? No.

The real enlightenment came when we talked about a phenomenon known as *spiritual open doors*. We covered topics such as the occult, types of divinations, sins, and forms of entertainment. That's the part that struck home with me: "entertainment". As a child, I use to sneak into the den while my parents were asleep and look at horror movies all night—to me, this was just innocent fun. I wouldn't go to bed until inundating my mind with images of gratuitous violence from movies like *A Nightmare on Elmstreet, Friday the 13th, Halloween, Hellraiser,* and more. At this point in the class the source of my demonic oppression became apparent. I opened a spiritual door to the demonic in my life through the medium of demonic entertainment. Satanic entertainment is a major source of much of the chaos we face today—it fills our minds with thoughts, images, concepts, and suggestions that make it difficult to operate with the mind of Christ. Darkness and filth attracts demons.

My visions and nightmares weren't of Freddy Krueger, Jason Voorhees, or Michael Myers, they were of spiders; but Freddy, Michael and Jason were instrumental in opening the doorway in my life for those arachnids (spirits) to reek havoc in my mind. But not all demons look and operate the same way.

HOLLYWOOD IMITATING REALITY

Demonology is nothing new. Throughout ancient times demons were regarded as the source of much mischief and strife in our world. From the fallen angels of Judaism, the jinn of Islam; the ferries, fauns and sylphs of Medieval literature; many bloodthirsty gods of Hinduism, the ancient Canaanite gods; the giant snakes, monstrous half-man, half-animal creatures of Babylonian mythology; the farfadets of ancient Mexico; to the succubus, incubus, demons and fallen angels of Christianity, every civilization has its demon-problem. Could this be a coincidence? Is it a coincidence that every civilization and culture on the face of the earth since the dawn of mankind has attributed the evils of our world to hordes of invisible entities? No. Our ancestors knew something that we're just now rediscovering in our time.

The most famous case of demonic possession in modern history came in 1953 when a young 17 year old Filipino girl named Clarita Villanueva was being bitten and choked by invisible entities. Two sets of teeth marks would press into her skin causing internal bleeding every-so-often. Bruises would mysteriously appear on her body. Clarita described to reporters present what she was seeing (she could see the entities, although others couldn't). She described one of the entities as being huge, very tall, covered with dark fur, possessing glowing red eyes, fangs, buck teeth, and wearing a cloak, and the other one as small (around 3 feet tall) and covered with fur, with sharp fangs. These entities would suddenly appear, chew all over her body, and then vanish. This may sound like a case of fantasy except for one thing: this would occur in the presence of medical doctors, nurses, news reporters, and prison guards. During this time, Clarita was a prison inmate in the Philippines, serving time for prostitution. The mauling was being witnessed by credible, trained observers. Professionals from all over the world were later called in to investigate what was going on with Clarita, and they were left dumbfounded and speechless by what they witnessed. The medical and scientific community, growing increasingly desperate, turned to the religious community for help. Representatives from different religions came with their amulets, incenses, books of prayers and incantations, etc., but nothing stopped the demonic attacks; and then, Dr. Lester Sumrall, a Christian evangelist heeding the call of the Holy Spirit to go only after fasting and praying, received permission by the government to visit Clarita and to pray for her. As was noted by reporters, the girl, upon seeing Dr. Sumrall, instantly shouted: "I hate you!!!" Dr. Sumrall, recognizing who was really talking, commenced to successfully casting out the demons. Newspapers all around the world wrote about the incident. It became one of the most widely documented cases of demonic possession in recent history.

There was another famous case of demonic possession after which the movie *The Exorcist* was based. The events in the movie were consistent with the Catholic Church's official report with only a few minor changes to the names, genders and locations.

Another highly popular case of demonic possession was adapted to the big screen in the 1980's: it was the case of a young woman who was repeatedly being sexually assaulted by a large invisible entity. The title of the movie was *The Entity*. This case, just like the one involving Clarita, was documented by credible observers: scientists and medical doctors. To this very day, no scientific explanation has been given that could explain the attacks that occurred.

Today, Hollywood is obsessed with demonic

possession. Every year they release movies based off of true life cases of demonic possession. It's big business! It also has a dangerous side. It has sparked an interest in the occult like never before. It has pulled on the curiosity of a generation who's inclined to believe in the supernatural, but aren't inclined to view this spirituality through the lens of the Bible. Like many people today love to proclaim: "I'm spiritual, but not religious." Without the correct understanding of this phenomenon, thrill-seekers will only end up getting sucked into a vortex of demonic deception and activity without knowing how to come out. The truth is this: demons are manifesting themselves in certain films, in many children's cartoons that are out today, and in most of today's music. Every pop, rock, and rap artist out today appears to be obsessed with the occult in their songs and music videos.

The main question is: Who are these demons and what do they really want? And how does all of this tie-in to our subject of giants? Some may even wonder if this is worth talking about. Well, I can assure you that it is, especially since much of the Bible talks about the need to learn how to fight invisible entities (demons and fallen angels) in what is known as spiritual warfare. The Apostle Paul even warned Christians about a breed of seducing spirits that will flood into the church and introduce "doctrines of demons" to the saints, thereby deceiving many into following a false Christianity in 1 Timothy 4:1.

WHAT ARE DEMONS, REALLY?

The most stated answer given to this question is: *demons are fallen angels*. But that's not the case. Understanding the identity of demons actually helps us to understand what David was up against when he faced Goliath, who the Bible refers to as a *Nephilim*. According to all of the early rabbinical sources and early church fathers, demons have a strange origin: they're the spirits of the deceased Nephilim. The Nephilim were the progeny of the angels (a type of angel known as a Watcher, found in Daniel 4:13, 17) who slept with human women. Genesis 6:4 says, "There were **giants** ("Nephilim") in the earth in those days; and also after that, when the **sons of God** (*B'nai HaElohim*) came in unto the **daughters of men** (*Bath Ha'adam*: daughters of *Adam*, meaning "mankind"), and they bare children to them, the same became mighty men which were of old, men of renown." *B'nai HaElohim* always refers to angels.

The arguments made against the angel-theory of the origin of the Nephilim don't really hold up theologically. The most popular theory of them all, which claims that the Nephilim were the offspring of unions between the sons of Seth and the daughter of Cain, is not Scripturally supported. Scripture describes these beings as staggeringly tall and strong (Amos 2:9), and very evil. They were non other than angel/human hybrids. Goliath was a later generation Nephilim whose height was 9 feet 11 inches. Goliath's coat of mail (chain-mail) was listed at five thousand shekels of brass (125–194lbs). Amazingly, just the iron blade of Goliath's spear by itself weighed an estimated 15lbs. So, we can only imagine how much his sword, helmet, and shield weighed. Goliath was a later generation Nephilim whose ancestors would have been genetically superior...and perhaps, bigger due to their genes not being as diluted as his.

Many rabbinical sources including the books of Enoch and Jasher, of which are specifically mentioned in the Old Testament, explained that the Nephilim, once destroyed by God during the Flood of Noah, and also afterwards when God sent the Israelites into the Land of Canaan to exterminate the remainder of them (Deuteronomy 9:1-3), were cursed by God to roam the earth as demon spirits, afflicting men and being exorcised by men. Basically, demons are the offspring of unions between angels and human women. Some have suggested that angels can't mate, and they cite Matthew 22:30 where Jesus said the saints, after receiving their new resurrected bodies, will be like the angels, neither marrying or being given in marriage; but what they are overlooking is the fact that Jesus never mentioned anything about the angels' ability to reproduce or at least engage in sexual activity; instead, Jesus was simply explaining that in heaven there will be no need for sexual activity. But, as is evidenced throughout Scripture, angels have been known to break the rules and engage in godless behavior. How else can you explain 1/3rd of the angels in heaven turning their backs on God and joining in rebellion alongside Lucifer to make war against God (Revelation 12:1), as well as the fact that many angels are currently locked-up in prisons in Tartarus, which is a department in hell, awaiting judgment because they *sinned against God* (2 Peter 2:4)? And Jude specifically lists the sins of these angels in verses 5 through 7, where he compared their sin to that of the people of Sodom who committed sexual perversion by seeking after "strange flesh" (a reference to the men of Sodom's attempt to rape two angels in Genesis 19:1-9)—only this time, instead of humans seeking the "flesh" of angels, it was the angels who sought after humans. I cover this in greater detail in my book *Exposing the Great Deception*.

SABOTAGE

Satan and his angels created the Nephilim for one reason: they wanted to sabotage God's plan to bring the Israelites into the Promised Land. Satan knew if he could block the Israelites from entering into the Land of Canaan, he could prevent the fulfillment of prophecy concerning the arrival of Jesus. For example, Jesus was prophesied to be born in Bethlehem; but had the Jews not occupied the Land of Canaan, this prophecy would not have been able to come to pass. How would Jesus have been able to ride into Jerusalem on a donkey as prophesied in Zechariah 9:9 if the Jews didn't occupy the land? Satan was only interested in sabotaging God's plans, which he already had knowledge of. When Satan puts giants in our paths, it's because he's attempting to prevent us from completing the assignment we were created to complete (Jeremiah 1:5; Ephesians 2:10). Yes, you were sent to this earth by God for a purpose. You are not an accident! Even Jesus' earthly lineage is filled with people born out of unfavorable circumstances like rape and incest, but none of that diminished the significance of Jesus' being nor affected His mission. The same is to be said about you. It doesn't matter so much how you got here; what matters is that you're here and you're here for a purpose. God knows this; Satan knows this; the demons assigned to your life by Satan knows this; everyone in the spiritual realm knows this; but the question is: Do you know this?

Knowing that you're not an accident, nor are you a cosmic coincidence (Evolution and Big Bang), but that you're a wonderfully handcrafted specimen designed by the Creator for a purpose in this world is the revelation you need to rightly understand why certain things happened in your life. Knowing that you were sent here for a purpose, Satan handcrafted just the right circumstances to derail you in life and get you off of your mission. Satan knew what areas in life you were called to conquer, and placed road-blocks in your way to redirect your course. Goliath is simply a road-block. His primary objective given by Satan is to cause you to shape a negative perception of yourself through traumatic experiences.

Goliath's mere appearance made the Israelite soldiers second-guess their God and their abilities.

They didn't even try to face Goliath. One sight of the giant made them run and hide. The Israelites, while in the dessert, didn't even attempt to enter into the Promised Land...after only *hearing* about the giants. What am I saying? Your giant is whatever alters your perception of yourself, causing you to feel small and insignificant. What altered your perception of yourself and took away your smile, zeal, passion, glow, and dream? What's the pivotal event in your life that put you on a destructive path or has you stagnated?

Mine was in the third grade. That was the year I was molested by a much older boy. That was the day I developed a perception of myself I would find myself wrestling with for years to come, even after I entered the ministry. The Bible never told us to pray away demonic strongholds (patterns of thinking); it said to "cast down" strongholds: thoughts and imaginations. And I had to learn that it didn't matter that I was an intercessor, a minister, and active in church; I still saw myself through the lens of that moment in my life; I was still affected by it, even unconsciously. I was angry and didn't know why. I carried a chip on my shoulder without understanding why. The trauma from that event stayed with me for years. Every so often I'd become entranced in an unsubstantiated and unwarranted spell of anger; my mind filled with violent images of revenge—a spiritual open door. It was time for me to confront that traumatic event by opening up about it and discussing it with others, by acknowledging it as well as the emotions that I felt as a result of that experience. Satan's strategy is to get individuals to hide and conceal situations rather than open up about them, confess them, bring them to the light and confront them out in the open. The Bible tells us it is only when we open up and confess our sins (actions and activities) that we can find the mercy and help that we need to overcome them in Proverbs 28:13. My healing began to occur the more I confessed, opened-up, and talked about the situation with others. I finally began to release the anger and un-forgiveness and confront the situation I had attempted to bury, and I began to regain power back over my own soul. You can't "cast down" that which you won't first acknowledge. You can't take authority over that which you won't confront. You can't get victory over that which you won't first bring to the light—out in the open. Denial and secrecy are tools used against your progress by demonic forces. Don't cover up anymore. Find an accountability partner or group of partners who're spiritually mature (Galatians 6:1) and open up today! Let them both pray for you and counsel you into health (Galatians 6:2; Hebrews 10:25). You're not a one-man army, you're a part of a body—a team (1 Corinthians chapter 12).

What's your pivotal event? Is it that rape that has you defensive and paranoid? Is it that moment when your mother called you a pest, or the one when your dad molested you? Is that why your self-esteem is the size of a grasshopper? Is it the moment your school teacher told you that you were slow, stupid, incorrigible, useless, and that you'd never be anything in life? Is it the moment they called you ugly? Is that why you're always so self-conscious and dubious of anyone that seems to be attracted to you, or you give-in to every man that calls you beautiful...as if you see no value in yourself? Is yours the moment that alcohol and/or drugs seized control of your life, and you lost control? Maybe it was the moment that you accomplished something great (graduated; won 1st place; etc.), but no one was there to celebrate you. Is that when you started viewing yourself as unimportant? What's causing you to measure your worth by comparing yourself to others? The game of "measurements" is Goliath's game. Whatever makes you feel insecure, insignificant, and unimportant, that is your giant; and it's not going anywhere; not, at least, until you put your war paint on and take the fight to it by confronting the incident with the revelation of its true source and purpose: it was sent by Satan to keep you stuck in yesterday, and to rob you of your purpose. What were you like *before* that pivotal moment? *That's what Satan stole.* It's time to get it back. Get your confidence, courage, zest, and dream back.

God's purpose and plan for your life is to put you in a position of wealth, prosperity and influence for the sake of glorifying Him in the earth (Jeremiah 29:11; 1 Kings 10). God desires to raise up not just you, but also your children to be bold ambassadors for His Kingdom in the earth. This is why one of the promises of God in Scripture is the promise to bless

69

your children and their children. In the 112th Psalm we find this concerning God's plan for your family:

> "Praise the LORD! How joyful are those who fear the LORD and delight in obeying his commands. Their children will be successful everywhere; an entire generation of godly people will be blessed. They themselves will be wealthy, and their good deeds will last forever. Light shines in the darkness for the godly. They are generous, compassionate, and righteous. Good comes to those who lend money generously and conduct their business fairly. Such people will not be overcome by evil. Those who are righteous will be long remembered. They do not fear bad news; they confidently trust the LORD to care for them. They are confident and fearless and can face their foes triumphantly. They share freely and give generously to those in need. Their good deeds will be remembered forever. They will have influence and honor" (NLT).

God wants to liberate you so that you, as well as your entire family, will possess the freedom to serve Him. It's not God's will that your household struggle with lack, poverty, defeat, dependence on the state and government, addictions, prison, sexual perversions, violence, and generational curses. There is more at stake than your personal comforts. Your ability to impact souls, your children's ability to impact souls, your ability to advance God's Kingdom and to prove to the world the magnitude of the God you serve is being impeded by the magnitude of the giant you've yet to face and defeat; and that giant won't stop with you; it will move on to your children also in order to alter their destinies, cut their lives short, place them on the path of destruction, and use them to advance Satan's kingdom in the earth.

Satan's big concern is that you'll begin to recognize that these pivotal moments in your life were strategically placed there by him for the purpose of stalling and derailing you—and that you're not their source. Furthermore, Satan is afraid you might decide to stop pitying yourself, stop hiding your pains, and start reclaiming the power over your life. Satan is more afraid of you discovering that you can regain this power through Christ, who strengthens us. The thing Satan needs the most in order to keep you in a state of bondage is to keep you blind to his schemes and to God's plans for your life (2 Corinthians 2:11). This is why Paul reveals to us in Ephesians 6:12 that we're "not fighting against flesh-and-blood enemies, but against evil rulers and authorities of the unseen world, against mighty powers in this dark world, and against evil spirits in the heavenly places." The moment that you realize you are a threat to hell and you stop perceiving yourself through the eyes of the enemy and start seeing yourself through God's eyes (Colossians 3:1-17), Goliath's knees will buckle.

CHAPTER 3 OBJECTIVES:

•Realize that mental torment doesn't come from God. God convicts us of sins, but He doesn't torment us with fear. Satan binds us with fear, shame, anxiety and depression, not God. That's demonic.

•Seek out classes in Bible colleges and/or churches and read Christian material on spiritual warfare.

•Ask God to reveal to you any and all open doors that might be in your life through which demonic spirits keep entering into your life (occult items, sins, forms of satanic entertainment, etc.)

•Intentionally revisit the past pains and traumas in your life (experiences, words, sights, etc.) and ask the Holy Spirit to give you the understanding and insight you need in order to perceive them correctly. Sit down with a Christian counselor during this process if needed. Write down your thoughts in a journal and read the Bible daily. As you read the Bible, you will begin to connect with the characters therein, seeing how they were hurt, wounded and affected by pains and traumas and how God was able to help them overcome them. Pray for God to heal you of every hidden thing in your heart and help you to release the hurt and pain from your heart. Forgive others and yourself. Don't use words and language that blames yourself—"If only I had of..." or "It's all because of me that..." Instead, speak these words: "God, I thank You that I am free from _____. I am no longer controlled by this. Today, I am a new creation in Jesus name, Amen."

Chapter 4

DOMINION

"If God be for us, who can be against us?"
—Romans 8:31

IT WAS THE 1995 GOLDEN GLOVES REGIONALS which were being held in South Carolina. I was preparing for my match when in walked into my locker room a young man to inform me about my opponent. He explained to me what I was up against: a 40-0 five-time Florida state champion. Sure enough, that was what I was up against. I was getting ready to jump into the ring with an undefeated Cuban kid with lightning fast hands and fancy feet...in only my second fight. The young man who entered into my locker room (where my coach and I were) was taken aback by one thing: my confidence. After informing me that my opponent was undefeated—and making him seem nearly unbeatable—my response was, "Well, this is his first loss tonight."

Round One: his lightning fast speed seemed quite overwhelming. His strategy was: combination, move; combination, move. He was difficult to keep up with. Round Two: I changed my strategy. *Go for the body, Timothy.* It worked! I found my sweetspot... and his weak spot. With each punch my confidence grew. Finally, my goal was no longer winning; it was now to prevent my opponent from being able to walk out of the ring in his own strength; it was now to ensure that he would have to be carried out of the ring and to the local hospital instead. In the middle of round two he was gasping for air, trying to breath; I was like a shark in bloody waters having a feeding frenzy. I didn't quite accomplish my goal of sending him to the local hospital, but I did walk away with a *unanimous decision* victory and a fulfilled promised to hand the undefeated fighter his first loss.

I appreciate my days in the ring. They taught me to appreciate winning and losing, the good days and the bad days; and more importantly, how to get up after being knocked down and regroup after being caught off-guard. Every promise of God comes with a fight. The devil is not going to just hand you the Promised Land...especially when considering he has worked so hard to sabotage your journey getting there. But the one thing that truly frightens the enemy is when a Believer comes ready to fight against him, and against their sinful urges and doubts. The enemy wishes you would just lie down and let him have a field day in your life, but be like the Apostle

Paul who declared, "Therefore I run in such a way, as not without aim; I box in such a way, as not beating the air; but I discipline my body and make it my slave, so that, after I have preached to others, I myself will not be disqualified" (1 Corinthians 9:26-27, NASB). Like athletes, we must discipline our minds to conform to the Word and discipline through repetition our bodies to submit to God's will. The Greek word for "discipline" used here is *hypōpiazō*, and it means "to beat black and blue; to beat one's body and handle it roughly; to discipline by hardships."

Like any good fighter, you must prepare for a fight before the actual fight. This stage entails preparing not only physically, but mentally as well. Serious fighters may go into seclusion so as to eliminate any and all distractions. They know the difficulty of fighting with a mind that's cluttered. When we look at the real ultimate fighter, Jesus, we see this demonstrated throughout His ministry: Jesus would isolate Himself quite often, going to the mountains to pray; He did this because He knew He had many devils to contend with down in the valley. Jesus would spend hours in prayer every morning before the sun came up; this is why it would take Him only a few seconds to knock out devils. The more time you spend with God, the more power you gain over satanic powers.

BE DIFFERENT

Joshua and Celeb were the only two men among the Israelites in the wilderness who were determined to not die in the wilderness. They knew that the desert was just a temporary stop on the road to something greater. *Keep in mind that there were nearly two million men and women in the Israelite camp.* The Bible says that Joshua and Caleb had a "different spirit" than the others (Numbers 14:24)—they had a fighting spirit and were willing to fight for the Promised Land; they were willing buck in the face of fear and fight to maintain their faith. Your faith is worth fighting for. The Israelites had just come off the heals of a major victory after not only witnessing God destroy the Egyptian army at the Red Sea, but also securing a major victory over the Amalekites. They witnessed too many miracles to suddenly believe God couldn't give them victory over the giants.

The confidence that these two men owned resulted from witnessing God in action. They weren't confident in their own abilities; they were confident in God's abilities. When they addressed the Israelite camp in an attempt to get them to press on with the conquest of the Land of Canaan rather than run in fear due to the report of the giants in the land, they reminded the people of God's power rather than the size of the giants. They knew that if the people could remember how big God is the people would become less concerned about how big the giants were. This is what Joshua and Caleb said in their address:

"They said to all the people of Israel, 'The land we traveled through and explored is a wonderful land! And if the LORD is pleased with us, he will bring us safely into that land and give it to us. It is a rich land flowing with milk and honey. Do not rebel against the LORD, and don't be afraid of the people of the land. They are only helpless prey to us! They have no protection, but the LORD is with us! Don't be afraid of them!'" (Numbers 14:7-9; NLT).

They didn't praise the giants at all—not one bit. They didn't even focus on the giants while speaking. They only talked about God—His power; His ability; His promise to them. They warned the people not to anger God. They emphasized that it was more needful for them to fear God's wrath rather than the giants' swords. This is how we develop the right confidence: by reminding ourselves of God's power, His ability, His promises. We must talk to ourselves about God, not our problems, and rest confidently in His ability. Do you talk to yourself? If so, what about? Do you focus more on what you feel (*I feel like God doesn't hear me; I feel like God doesn't care; I feel like I am a failure; I feel...*) or focus on what you know (*I know I am victorious, more than a conqueror, and that God hears my prayers...because His Word says so!*)? Focus on what you know, not how you feel. Speak it daily.

Satan is able to deceive people into speaking defeat into their lives by distorting their perceptions of God. His number one lie is: God is behind all of the evil in the world today. This is untrue because in the book of Genesis it was Adam who gave Satan authority over the earth to exercise his authority; and as Jesus explained, Satan's desire is to kill, steal, and destroy (John 10:10). God urges us to walk in His love. His Commandments (Exodus 20:1-17) outlaw practices such as murder, stealing, lying, adultery (which produces broken homes and contributes to much of society's breakdown), dishonoring parents, and desiring other people's possessions (covetousness, which leads to disrespect, retaliation, and violence). God outlawed practices such as chattel slavery (in Exodus chapter 21, it was a crime in ancient Israel to kidnap and purchase kidnapped individuals, treat servants with cruelty, rape, split-up homes, and even view servants as property as explained in Leviticus 25:39-40, among other things). God established property laws (Exodus chapter 22) and laws that prohibited things such as human sacrifices, sex slavery, and prostitution (Leviticus chapter 18). Jesus even said to love and pray for your enemies in Matthew chapter 5. These are just a few of the many laws in the Bible that foster respect, civility, a good work habit, honesty, freedom, and happiness in society. The opposite is what Satan offers. *There is a reason why the founding forefathers of America relied on the Bible as the basis for our laws and our Constitution.* The other lie that Satan loves to use on us is: God doesn't love you. The truth is: just because God doesn't do what we want Him to do, that does not mean He doesn't love us. That's a dangerous rationale to have: a belief that if someone loves you they will never say no to you. Sometimes it is a blessing to have someone tell you no. A "no" might save your life. In reality, a person who truly loves you will tell you the hurtful truth...in a loving way. But the proof of God's love is found in the fact that He sent His own Son, Jesus, to die for our sins so that we could be reconciled to Himself. As John 3:16 says, God so loved the world that He gave us salvation through His Son on the cross...but God so respects free-will that He refuses to force us to accept His Son's atonement for our sins. It's our decision to receive salvation. Also, God doesn't wait for us to earn His love. We can't! As Paul wrote in Romans 5:8, "But God showed his great love for us by sending Christ to die for us while we were still sinners" (NLT). God wants you as you are so that He can make you into the person He designed you to be. He doesn't judge you for your mistakes, and He doesn't hate you because of your sins. He loves you enough to convict you of sin and bless you through your mistakes. So, when you talk about God, do so with the correct understanding of His love and will for you (Malachi 3:16).

Have confidence in God. He performs miracles for us simply to prove to us He is able to do what He promised in our lives. Don't look to yourself for strength. Don't place confidence in your ability. This is why God let you get placed on the backside of the desert where the castaways are located: so He could prove to you that He is your protector and provider. This is why God took you the route that He did: just to show you that He'll open the doors for you even when men say you can't do *it* or achieve *it*. Like God told the Israelites in Deuteronomy 8:18, He will give us the ability to get wealth; His only condition being one thing: don't claim you "made it" because of your wits, smarts, education, networks and abilities. Give God all of the glory and the credit. Brag on God!

Joshua and Caleb were confident in God, not themselves. Sadly, they were the only ones with this confidence. The rest of the Israelites were looking at their puny frames and comparing them to the enormous frames of the giants. The people grew angry at the thought of even challenging the giants. The Bible says, "But the whole community began to talk about stoning Joshua and Caleb. Then the glorious presence of the LORD appeared to all the Israelites at the Tabernacle. And the LORD said to Moses, 'How long will these people treat me with contempt? Will they never believe me, even after all the miraculous signs I have done among them?'" (Numbers 14:10-11; NLT). God had to stop the Israelites from stoning Joshua and Caleb. We must not allow challenges to frighten us out of obeying God; instead, we must allow our faith in God to frighten us out of yielding to fear. We should fear doubting God...especially after He's proven Himself over and over again.

Doubt is a momentum killer. Faith comes by hearing the Word of God; therefore, doubt comes by hearing arguments that contradict the Word of God. Doubt and faith are byproducts of what we hear daily. We choose what we listen to. Faith produces miracles; doubt produces no miracles. If you're in need of a miracle, listening to individuals who don't believe in the miracle working power of God and also filling your mind with things that aren't conducive to spiritual growth will only decrease your chances of receiving a miracle. There are things God placed in our power to do—choosing to believe Him is one.

HOW FAITH WORKS

Faith is activated through an act of obedience. When the Bible says, "Faith without works is dead" (James 2:26), it's not saying faith plus good deeds and social activism is what's required of us; it's saying that faith plus obedience to God's specific instructions is what's needed. We must hear and obey what God is telling us. "Works" in context simply refers to obedience to that which God is telling us to do in a particular situation. When Paul talked about faith in Romans 10:17, he said that faith comes by hearing, and hearing by the "word" of God. In the Greek, "word" is translated as *rhema* in this passage, and *rhema* is defined as "that which is or has been uttered by the living voice; a thing spoken; word." In other words, faith is not only based off of that which is written in the Word of God, but also that which is spoken to us by God at the precise moment. Jesus said we must not live by bread alone, but by every "word" (*rhema* in the Greek) that proceeds from the mouth of God in Matthew 4:4. This means God is still speaking today. God has given us a Bible to read and get basic instructions concerning His will for us, but He has also given us prophets and other ministers to speak directly into our lives at different moments and in different situations. The Bible already instructs us to work if we want to eat, but it doesn't say whether or not you need to accept that job being offered to you from another state or you should apply at that company down the street. For specific instructions that pertain to your individual situation, you need a rhema word. Taking the wrong job could be a deadly mistake. You know it's not good to be alone from reading Genesis chapter two, but concerning whether or not Johnny or Mike is the man that you should marry, you need a rhema word so that you will know what you should do in that particular situation. God delivers a rhema word through the Holy Spirit and His prophets.

When my wife and I were seeking God for direction concerning our living arrangement—during that time, we were living in a property that we were not happy with—we did what the Bible teaches us as Christians to do regarding decisions: we went on a fast and we prayed. It was one Friday evening that we visited a church during this time and we received just what we needed: a rhema word. An usher, full of the Holy Spirit (you don't have to hold the office of a prophet in order to prophecy according to 1 Corinthians chapter 12), stopped us and prophesied to us while we were leaving out the door. She spoke, "God said, 'Don't move. He's working something out for you.'" Then she went on to share some more things with my wife and I that God was speaking regarding our situation, and she was completely accurate. She didn't know me and that I was in the middle of contemplating whether or not I should sell the property and move. That was a rhema word. God had to send me a *rhema* since there was no Bible verse that said, "Thou shalt not sell thine house, Timothy-eth."

In the Old Testament, whenever the kings of ancient Israel wanted to know which direction they should take regarding a matter, they would consult the prophets of the Lord. They knew the importance of receiving divine guidance before making important decisions. We must live by the *rhema* of God. In some situations, kings were misled by false prophets because their hearts were hard-hearted towards the Lord (1 Kings 22:5-28); in other cases, kings turned to pagan priests and prophets of false gods like Baal and suffered as a result thereof. There are examples of God not speaking to some men due to their deliberate disobedience (as was the case with king Saul in 1 Samuel chapter 28), and even refusing to speak to the Nation of Israel due to their decision to worship idols as revealed in Amos 8:11. So, adhering to the instructions in righteousness found in the written Word (Bible; *logos*) is important for setting us up to receive a rhema word—to put it another way: before

God reveals to us specific instructions, we must first be willing to obey His written instructions.

ACTUALLY, FAVOR IS FAIR

The first step towards developing a godly confidence is obedience to God's commandments. The Bible, in 1 John 3:20-22, tells us that when we are living under a conviction of sin, that conviction is an indication that God is active in our lives; and when we are free from conviction due to our repentance and obedience to His commandments, then we have the confidence to ask God for anything in prayer, knowing that He will hear us. Pleasing God by obeying Him gives us a level of confidence in prayer that is needed in order to pray boldly and effectively. Here is an important revelation: God loves everyone equally—there's no variance when it comes to His love for us—but He does have favorites (Acts 10:34-35; John 9:31; James 5:16). We determine whether or not we receive God's favor by our choices and actions.

The Israelites, while in the wilderness, knew that they were being disobedient to God and living in deliberate sin. Knowing that God wasn't pleased with them, some of the Israelites decided that they were going to possess the Land of Canaan with their own might as opposed to God's (Numbers 14:40). They ended-up being slaughtered. When we're obedient to God, we're able to walk in His might, which means He'll go ahead of us and ensure that we have the victory in situations, but when we refuse to obey

God and choose not to wait for Him to give us the instruction to pursue something, and we pursue after it anyway using our own might, God will not be with us, and we'll find ourselves defenseless.

When Joshua and the Israelites were in battle against Ai, they were overconfident and thought they could easily secure a victory in their own strength. Joshua and the Israelites didn't even bother sending their entire army due to the fact that Ai's army was only a fraction of the size of theirs, but the Israelites' arrogance came back to haunt them because Ai was able to whip and drive them back. The Israelites couldn't understand how just a few days earlier they were able to defeat armies much larger than Ai, but now they were unable to defeat an army a fraction of the size of the ones they defeated. They forgot that their previous victories in battle were the result of God's favor, not their military might. Similarly, America has fallen into the same trap of arrogance, thinking just because we were able to defeat enemies in the past with our military might, we will be able to defeat the ones up ahead of us. But if God removes His hand from America, even the smallest band of rebels can defeat the mighty U.S.A. We can't afford to be arrogant and lose the favor of God.

When Joshua and the Israelites got to the real root of the problem—after discovering that their defeat came not because of poor military skills, poor timing, and poor weaponry, but because they didn't obey God's instruction to avoid taking the spoils of

Jericho after their defeat—they quickly attacked the problem: they found Achan, the man that disobeyed God's instruction and brought a curse on the people as a whole, and then killed both he and his family; and afterwards, when they went up against Ai for a second time, they won the battle. Victory for Believers comes from walking in God's favor, and this favor only comes from obeying God's Word.

Get rid of the root problem that leads to defeat: a rebellious spirit towards God. We can't rebel against God and expect to be blessed by Him at the same time. We have to ask God to give us an obedient spirit. Being submissive to God doesn't mean submitting to every leader. Some people—including individuals within leadership in the church—will sometimes instruct Christians to do things that are unbiblical...and blatantly sinful; in those situations, obeying God entails disobeying that leader. In some cases, parents will instruct their kids to commit sin. All children, once at the age of accountability (Isaiah 7:16), must decide whether or not they are going to obey God or disobey God by obeying their parents' sinful requests. Jesus stated in Matthew 10:37: if we love our parents—or anyone else for that matter—more than Him, then we are not worthy of Him. So, loving God may mean disappointing people close to us, as well as those who are in positions of authority over us. We'll all stand before God in judgment one day, and no one will be able to advocate on our behalves. *Know that no one is worth going to hell over.*

WHEN GOD SAYS GO

Once God has spoken to you and given you a rhema word, it's time for you to set out on the journey. The way you begin the journey is how you must finish it. For example, if you jumped into a situation because God instructed you to, then you must continue to rely on God's guidance in that situation. If God told you to open-up a car lot, then you have to continue to walk with Him through intimate prayer if you're going to succeed with that car lot. If you received a supernatural healing from God for your body, you must remain in Christ and under His power in order to keep that healing. Paul said in Galatians 3:1-5 that if we start the process following the Holy Spirit, we must complete the task following the Holy Spirit. We can't begin with prayer and fasting and seeking after God's guidance, and then halfway through the journey switch and start relying on our friends, our intellect, our smarts, and our resources to finish the journey. *We tend to ditch God bout' halfway through.*

The Israelites were delivered out of Egypt supernaturally, sustained in the desert supernaturally; therefore, the only way they were going to seize the Land of Canaan from the giants was to rely on that same supernatural power which gave them repeated victories. Sadly, because they were hesitant to move forward when God said go, and due to their reluctance to trust God the rest of the way, God cursed them to remain—and die—in the desert; God then took their children into the Promised Land...along with Joshua and Caleb, who were the only two men that were confident in God. Some instructions God give us are time sensitive, which basically means we can't move when we get ready; we must move exactly when God says move. Wait too long and you may miss your opportunity. Contrary to popular belief, what God has for us will not always be available to us. The Bible even tells us to seek God *while He may be found*...because even His presence will not always be available to us. The opportunity to surrender our lives to Christ and receive His salvation is over once we're in our graves. If the Holy Spirit is pressing you to start a business, write a book, relay a message to someone, pray and intercede for certain person, sow a seed, go to a certain location or not go to a certain location, call a certain person or even leave a certain person, then do it when He tells you to because it's a time-sensitive matter. Evangelist Reinhard Bonnke, in his testimony, talked about how God asked him to be a missionary in Africa, preparing those in that land for a end-times visitation of God. He said God wanted him to answer *yes* because the situation was time-sensitive. He shared that God told him that He had asked three other people before him and they all said no. In another incident Reinhard talked about a situation where he was dying while in the land and, at that precise moment, God prompted a woman in another country to start praying for him. God specifically told the woman to rebuke the spirit of death off of Reinhard. She had no idea that he was on his death bed at the time, but she obeyed; and because of her obedience, the spirit of death was banished and Evangelist Bonnke's life was miraculously spared. In one incident, a woman, on the day of September 11, 2001, was awakened extra early that morning and instructed to pray by the Holy Spirit. She began to pray, and while praying, sensed that something terrible was going to happen that day. She testified that God told her to not let her husband go in to the office that day—he worked in one of the towers that was destroyed that day. She didn't know how to tell her husband she had a bad feeling about him going in to work on that day, so she creatively stopped him from going in to the office: she rewinded the hand on the clock back several hours so that he wouldn't wake-up on time and get to the office on time. After waking-up and discovering what time it was, he became upset with his wife's scheming; but later, being late was the last thing on his mind...after he and his wife watched in horror the planes smashing into the World Trade Center Towers where he worked...and where he would have been had his wife not heeded the warning of the Holy Spirit that morning. One morning, while my wife was seeking work, the Holy Spirit placed a certain individual in her spirit to call. She had never reached out to this person before, but out of obedience she called them. She didn't know that this person, who she'd just recently met, was an employer that was, at that precise moment, looking for someone to fill a position that had just become vacant due to a firing. Had my wife called any earlier or any later than she did, she would have missed that blessing. God is a God of timing.

When we step out on faith (meaning do what God tells us to do when He speaks to us), that's when God will begin to open up the doors and provide the funds, people, and resources. God never shares with us all of the details up front. He shares information with us as we go. The key is to seek God for every instruction in the process. Never get cocky and think you can take things into your own hands and finish the task without hearing from God each step of the way. It's not about the journey, nor the task, nor is it about the destination; it's about the process.

GO DOMINATE!

Confidence comes when we know that we are walking in God's will. We dominate in God's might and where God tells us to, and with what God gives us. There is no competition in the place where God has given you dominion. It doesn't matter how big Goliath is; his defeat is already predestined by God. *The fight is fixed!* The only card Goliath has to play is the intimidation card. Sure, the price of the property is intimidating, your lack of credentials is intimidating, the enormity of the responsibility is intimidating, the risks and liabilities are intimidating, and the task is big, but you have a guaranteed victory if God has declared it's yours. God's promise isn't a gamble; it's the surest guarantee we'll ever have. Go forward!

CHAPTER 4 OBJECTIVES:

•Brag on God today. Spend the entire day talking to yourself and to other people about how awesome, powerful, mighty and loving God is.

•Refrain from dwelling on negative thoughts and using negative words today. If something bad happens or something isn't going right, simply say, "I know God is going to fix it," or declare to yourself through prayer: "I put this in Your hands God and I thank You that You're going to fix it for Your glory today, in Jesus name, Amen."

•I dare you to think about that which isn't going right and pray, "Lord Jesus, I thank You even in the midst of this (state what the problem is). For, all things are still working together for my good." Practice thanking God even in your hardships.

•Ask God for a rhema word. Also, ask God to confirm His Word to you through other ministers. The Bible says that in the mouths of two or three witnesses God will establish a thing (2 Corinthians 13:1).

•Change your speech. Rather than taking credit for the good things, accomplishments and successes in your life, say, "God allowed me to do or accomplish _____." Give God the credit, but not for sinful pursuits, though. With regards to sinful things and pursuits, attribute those to Satan and your fleshly, sinful nature and ask God to help you abstain from those things that are displeasing to Him.

•Ask God for wisdom to walk in His instructions.

ONE GIANT AWAY

CHAPTER 5

UNCONVENTIONAL

*"We use God's mighty weapons, not worldly
weapons, to knock down the strongholds
of human reasoning and to destroy false
arguments."—2 Corinthians 10:4 (NLT)*

DURING THE 1980'S, AN EPIDEMIC of unspeakable violence swept throughout the
nation of Uganda, Africa. This crime wave
was unusual because it involved open, heavy witchcraft. A movement emerged known as the Lord's Resistance Army (LRA), created by a powerful witch
doctor who believed they were in contact with Jesus. This false Christ convinced this medium that
they needed to create an army that would stamp
out evil in the land. The irony is: the LRA was the
ultimate engineer of the evil that gripped the land.
They engaged in countless raids on innocent citi-
zens, mutilating and butchering them with machet-

es, knives and bullets, and routinely kidnapped children to use as child soldiers. They trained children to murder, to rape, to cannibalize, and to do other unspeakable acts of horror. Each child was baptized in evil, being anointed by their witch doctor leader, Joseph Kony, who would regularly consult with demon spirits for guidance. The supernatural element began to manifest when the Ugandan military tried to intervene and put an end to the LRA. Oftentimes, the military would have the LRA surrounded, but the LRA would seemingly supernaturally evade them and escape capture. Most times, the LRA would know when the military was about to attack, where they were mobilizing, and what their plan of action was. Kony would receive advanced warnings from his demon guides ahead of time. For years the Ugandan military was ineffective in capturing the LRA despite being superiorly armed and far outnumbering them. The slaughters continued. The raids continued. The horror continued. Many child soldiers, at the behest of the spirits, were instructed to slaughter their own parents. No one was safe. The Christian churches, though optimistic at first that God was going to put a stop to the LRA and bring back their children, began to slowly lose hope. Great fear began to grip the pastors and their members. The authorities and the military couldn't stop this sadistic band of vicious killers; but finally, the church there in Uganda began to seek the Lord through prayer and fasting for a solution to the problem. God began to speak to the pastors and intercessors there, revealing to them the true source of the problem. He revealed to them that what they were up against was an enemy more deadly than anything physical: they were up against powerful witchcraft. God began to reveal to the pastors that before they could defeat the power of the LRA they had to first repent of their own witchcraft. Christians began tossing their amulets, their charms and oils, their incenses, their books of spell, and all other tools of the occult into the fire, burning them; afterwards, the military and government, in a joint effort to seek out and destroy the LRA, followed the instructions of God and went to the sacred places where Joseph Kony's altars were. Kony would go to those altars to commune with demons. They served as a type of spiritual power grid. At one of the sacred spots there was a pool of sacred water that had been consecrated by Kony. Soldiers reported that when leaves landed in or even flew over that pool of water, they would die instantly right before their eyes. The water was so cursed it was poisonous. The pastors began praying over those sacred spots, pleading the blood of Jesus over them and rebuking the powers of Satan from them. They demolished all of the cursed items at those altars just like God told the Israelites to do when they entered the Promised Land. After destroying these altars, idols, and leading the entire nation in the repentance of not only their witchcraft but also the witchcraft of their ancestors, the first rays of light began to break through the dark cloud of tyranny and fear. Ugandan military troops began capturing and killing LRA leaders and detaining the child soldiers. As the church continued to pray and walk in repentance, Kony's very own generals testified that Kony expressed to them in frustration that the demons were leaving and that he couldn't seem to get any guidance from them anymore. Due to prayer and repentance, the demonic powers that fueled the LRA were weakening...and the LRA was starting to lose the battle. But the miracles didn't end there. In the coming weeks and months, children who had been kidnapped were suddenly beginning to return home to their parents. Through the power of God the spells over them had been broken, even to the point that their compulsions to kill were lessening. Droves of military soldiers gave their lives to Christ behind this ordeal—after all, they had just witnessed first hand the power of witchcraft and the power of God. They realized that demons are real, that God is real, that Jesus is more powerful than any demon and witch, and the Christians who walk in the power of God can drive back the driving forces behind all manner of evil. Guns weren't effective; prayer and repentance was.

What Uganda went through is no different than what the ancient Israelites went through. They had to discover that conventional weapons can't defeat demonic powers. God revealed to Moses that all of the evils in the Land of Canaan were the result of demonic influence. God revealed to the Israelites that the evil in the land was a result of the gods that had been given authority over the land through the sins of fornication and idolatry in Leviticus chapter eighteen. God revealed to the Israelites that the key to defeating evil was to cut the head off of the snake (Satan) by dethroning his idols. God warned the Israelites that if they failed to remove the idols of the false gods and to banish those who worshiped them from the land upon entering it, those idols and their worshipers would influence them and lead them to their own destruction. Psalm 106:34-41 says,

> "Israel failed to destroy the nations in the land, as the LORD had commanded them. Instead, they mingled among the pagans and adopted their evil customs. They worshiped their idols, which led to their downfall. They even sacrificed their sons and their daughters to the demons. They shed innocent blood, the blood of their sons and daughters. By sacrificing them to the idols of Canaan, they polluted the land with murder. They defiled themselves by their evil deeds, and their love of idols was adultery in the LORD's sight. That is why the LORD's anger burned against his people, and he abhorred his own special possession. He handed them over to pagan nations, and they were ruled by those who hated them." (NLT)

Notice the progression of events here: first, the people disobeyed God; second, they intermingled with idol worshipers (this represents the great compromise taking place in today's churches, as they prefer to abandon the truth of God's Word just to fit in and be politically correct; be accepting of other religious beliefs and include pagan gods in the house of God); third, they began sacrificing their own children on the altars of these idols (one of these gods was a god named Molech, and he was the god of abortion...as women who were desirous to get rid of their babies would sacrifice them in the fires of Molech, roasting them alive. Abortion is an act of idol worship); and fourth, they began to embrace more and more evil and commit more evil deeds; and lastly, God handed them over to their enemies to be ruled by them (ancient Israel lost its freedom and became a nation of slaves).

CONFUSION IN THE CAMP

Many people believe that they have an answer to all of the problems plaguing our society today. Everyone claims to have a solution. The world's answer to the problems in our society are: more education and more social programs. The solutions being given are a byproduct of evolutionary, socialist, atheistic, and Marxist philosophies. Evolution and atheism shuns any mention of a spiritual element in society's ills. Furthermore, Marxism and Socialism takes the humanist road and espouse the view that every problem in society is created by social conditions, and can therefore only be solved using social programs. Karl Marx, the engineer of Marxism and the father of Communism—and its offspring, Socialism—believed that the source of the world's evil is...property ownership. In a purely communist society, property ownership is forbidden since, according to Marx, it is the cause of such vices as greed, jealousy, murder, stealing, lying, and more. According to Marx, wealthy men who were land owners designed a system of servitude and placed men and women on their lands to work for them. In order to keep these men and women subservient, they created government for the purpose of forcing them to work their lands and then created religion for the purpose of manipulating the "working class" into loving their servitude. That's also why Communism outlaws religion. In perfect Communism, the goal is to eventually abolish all government, believing that if you get rid of property ownership you won't need a government, jails, police officers, judges, etc. because all evil will have been vanquished. Socialists operate in a fairytale world, believing that human nature is innately good and all mankind has to do to correct this world is to unify the whole of the human race. They're ignorant or willfully ignorant of the fact that human nature is plagued by a disease called sin; so, it doesn't matter if a person gets a degree, moves out of the ghetto and into a wealthy neighborhood, get a lot of money and a good paying job, and get married; they'll still carry inside of them the propensity and tendency to murder, oppress, treat unjustly, enslave, rape, steal, lie, and commit all manner of evil. The saddest part, however, is the fact that the Christian pastors today are espousing the same lies that the Marxists, humanists, Socialists, Communists, evolutionists, and atheists espouse. Some pastors are even laughing at the belief that demon spirits are a major contributor to the evils in our world. We have unbelieving Believers in our pulpits today—2 Peter chapter 2 said we would. If the church refuses to acknowledge that the root problem is spiritual and the solution is spiritual, not social, then the world will remain in serious trouble. When social activism replaces prayer meetings and activities like prayer and fasting are perceived as archaic and irrelevant; when the church believes it must embrace the progressivism of the day (progressive theology, moral relativism, situational ethics, etc.), that's when the enemy will be able to operate in the earth unopposed.

Satan's goal is the secularization of the church for the purpose of diminishing its power in prayer. The confusion that Christians face today is the issue of whether or not prayer still works. Some wonder if prayer ever worked. Children in America are taught to believe Christianity had no involvement in making this nation great. Political Correctness has effectively neutralized the church, scaring it out of taking a side on any of the sinful and destructive policies being made today. We quote 2 Chronicles 7:14 often but don't believe it, nor practice it—not the majority of us within Christendom today. No one wants to go to the throne of grace and intercede for the nation; and don't get me wrong, there are Christians who're praying and fasting and sounding the alarm, but not many. The majority are wallowing in confusion, trying to decide whether or not to listen to man's opinion or God's Word. This leads me to my next point:

AMERICAN IDOLS

Idolatry is rampant in the western world, and in no place is idolatry more rampant—and secretive—than in America, the land of the free and the home of the brave. It is no secret that America has a secret past. There were real genuine Christians who were involved in America's founding, but there were also several founding forefathers who were deeply involved in the occult. For example, President George Washington, America's first president, was a Master Mason who, during a masonic ceremony, dedicated America to the constellation Virgo. The practice of astrology and star-worship was strictly forbidden by God in the book of Deuteronomy chapter eighteen. Other leaders in American history, such as Benjamin Franklin, were heavily involved in occult circles. Several American presidents were members of the controversial Bavarian Illuminati spin-off group known as the Skull & Bones; others are participants of the festivities that take place at the highly secretive Bohemian Grove resort in California where an event known as the Cremation of Care takes place. During this event, presidents, congressmen, senators, media leaders, and a gang of other elites pray to a forty-foot stone owl known as the Owl of Minerva in Greek mythology. This god was known as the god of wisdom. These men even reenact a human child sacrifice by taking the effigy of a baby and tossing it into a fire at the foot of the stone idol. The biggest idol in Washington is the 6,666 foot tall obelisk known as the Washington Monumental sitting right in the heart of Washington D.C. And speaking of Washington D.C.—whose layout was specifically designed to create an image of an owl and a pentagram—what does the "D.C." stand for anyway? Well, it means "District of Columbia". That may not sound very troubling at first, not until you discover who Columbia is. Columbia is a derivative of the ancient Canaanite god Ashterah, which was the female counterpart of the Canaanite god Baal; so, the district belonging to Columbia may as well be aptly called the district dedicated to Ashterah/Baal. All of these things were put into place by the super secretive Freemasons.

A few short years ago, there was a prayer group who, armed with this knowledge, began praying over the sacred spots in Washington D.C. They went to these spots and began praying against the demonic powers given authority over the land as a result of the contracts made with them by certain of our founding fathers. Shortly afterwards, an unbelievable thing happened: a rare earthquake shook Washington D.C. No real damage was done to any of the structures in the area...except for one: the Washington Monumental (obelisk). What does an obelisk represent you ask? It is a religious item from ancient Egyptian mythology which represents the Egyptian god Osiris. To be blunt, it represents the phallus (genitalia) of Osiris. According to myth, Isis, Osiris' wife/sister, created the phallus (obelisk) and attached it to Osiris' dead body and then impregnated herself with it, thereby giving birth to Horus, the god whose eye sits in the capstone found above the pyramid sitting on the back of the dollar bill. Amazingly, the base of that obelisk in Washington was cracked during the earthquake. I believe in my heart that this was God letting the nation know that there are some idols and sacred spots dedicated to demons in America that need to be cast down if this nation is to ever get to the root of the gang problem, the drug problem, the sexual perversion problem, the racism problem, the economic problem, and every other problem plaguing the land. The church needs to get back to prayer and repentance if we're going to see the giants in this land overthrown. We need God's favor and protection again. We need the power of God to rest over the land once more.

UNCONVENTIONAL WARRIORS

David had to come up on the backside of the desert

so that he could learn how to fight an enemy that was supernatural in nature...literally. He had to fight an angel-human hybrid with a bad attitude. As Paul declared in Ephesians 6:12, "For we are not fighting against flesh-and-blood enemies, but against evil rulers and authorities of the unseen world, against mighty powers in this dark world, and against evil spirits in the heavenly places" (NLT). There is a place for conventional weapons (guns, etc.) as outlined in Romans 13:4, but you can't kill demons with bullets, fight ideologies with guns, and change hearts with governmental legislation. Until the heart is changed, the spirit is reconciled to God, and the mind is converted by the truth, the root problem will never be corrected; and until the root is dealt with, the symptoms will always keep returning, sometimes with a vengeance.

David learned in the desert that his weapon wasn't a slingshot, a spear, a sword, and a shield; his weapon was faith. As David discerned, "The LORD who rescued me from the claws of the lion and the bear will rescue me from this Philistine!" (1 Samuel 17:37). David regarded God as his rescuer, his deliverer, his protector. David learned how to access this weapon in the desert. David learned that faith can defeat fear, depression, anger, confusion, and low self-esteem; this weapon was able to deliver David from the mouth of discouragement and despair; this weapon gave him victory over a lion and a bear, and it was going to give him victory over a giant; he learned how to wield his faith in the desert: how to hear the voice of God; how to enter into the secret place through worship; how to access and operate in the anointing of God; how to speak the Word of God and employ God's angels (Psalm 103:20); how to rely on God and walk in divine confidence; how to hear and follow God's specific instructions. David knew these are the weapons God provides to His warriors. When David threw that stone, it was the Holy Spirit who increased its velocity and guided it supernaturally right between the eyes of Goliath—it wasn't the stone and the sling; it was God's power.

There are back-desert warriors being trained up at this hour: people who are overlooked, but are powerful because they are spending time with God; people who are perfecting the art of fighting in the spirit while the many other *conventionally religious* individuals are spending their time learning how to fight with man-made tools such as philosophy, rationalism, social activism, politics, ecumenicalism, inter-faith-ism, useless religious traditions, and other similar devices. Back-desert warriors attend the School of the Spirit, learning how to fight in the spirit realm; how to identify the real source behind the "symptoms" of crime, addictions, economic and educational problems, etc. plaguing our societies; they know how to banish the demon out of the gang member then insulate them with the love of God; they know how to follow the Holy Spirit as He gives them wisdom to deal with different situations; how to minister to the whole man (spirit, body and soul) and bring wholeness, not just healing; they know how to bind the "strongman" and loose deliverance into the situation through prayer, gentleness, truth, and love; they walk into hospitals and empty them out; they go into prisons and set inmates free from mental and spiritual prisons; they operate in the supernatural power of God and leave the jaws of medical doctors, lawyers, Naturalists, and others on the floor. Back-desert warriors are in the trenches; they end-up in palaces they didn't prepare for, standing before greatness; they are unconventional, dancing over the presence of God without a care in the world of who's looking, desiring to build God's house before even their own, and never losing their worship no matter how high up the ladder they climb.

UNCONVENTIONAL MEANS OF ELEVATION

Only David was anointed to face Goliath. Had any other man in the Israelites' camp stepped out to face the giant from Gath they would've been destroyed, not because they weren't using the proper weapons, but because they weren't anointed by God for that particular challenge. God was preparing David for the throne at that time when Goliath was taunting the Israelite army, and God needed a way to place the young lad into the spotlight for King Saul to notice him. God was grooming David to be Saul's replacement. Before the arrival of Goliath, David was unknown, even by his own kin; therefore, God used a giant problem to give David a giant spotlight just so he'd end-up gaining recognition from the king.

What presented itself as a big challenge really was an opportunity for elevation. God was using Goliath to elevate David to the king's house. The prize king Saul was offering to any man that could kill the giant was his daughter's hand in marriage; so, by David killing Goliath, he practically became part of the king's family...alongside gaining great fame. David ended-up in the palace through unconventional means; he wasn't born in affluence, didn't go to a big name school, didn't undergo training in the art of conventional warfare; he wasn't even perceived as kingly material by his own father when the prophet Samuel went to Jesse's house to anoint the next king of Israel in secret. David wasn't skilled at everything—a jack of all trades; an expert on every subject; highly lauded as a great one. David was just skilled at...trusting God...and anointed for this moment; and a problem took David to a place (a palace) and placed him directly under greatness ahead of all of his brothers who dreamed and trained for it. One obtacle changed David's entire life, taking him from the backside of the desert to the king's palace overnight—just one! Never underestimate a problem. Never overlook the blessings that problems bring. Quite often we perceive trouble as a hindrance to our progress, but trouble may just be the catalyst for true progress in our lives. God may be sending the next level of blessings for your life in the package of problems. Remember this: The bigger the problem, the bigger the opportunity; the bigger the opportunity, the higher the elevation.

James explains the importance of not letting trouble derail our faith and cause us to become negative when confronted with challenges, things that derail our plans, and the unexpected curve balls life throws our way. James wrote, "Dear brothers and sisters, when troubles come your way, consider it an opportunity for great joy. For you know that when your faith is tested, your endurance has a chance to grow. So let it grow, for when your endurance is fully developed, you will be perfect and complete, needing nothing" (James 1:2-4; NLT). James called trouble an opportunity to grow spiritually, to develop spiritually, and to mature and to become great.

Are you facing a huge problem today? If so, then it might be God interrupting your affairs so that He can shift your life to another level. God brought just the right challenge your way, and then gave you the perfect weapon to defeat it at just the right moment in your life. Now isn't the time to complain, and it's certainly not the time to run; but rather, this is the time to rejoice, employ your faith, believe and expect a miracle, knowing that "all things" are working for your good—your problems are really God setting you up for elevation. Let God show Himself strong in you. There's only one person anointed for this giant: you. This isn't your problem; it's your opportunity. Take it!

CHAPTER 5 OBJECTIVES:

•Read the Bible to get an understanding of the spiritual causes behind every earthly problem.

•Denounce any and all idols you may have in your life. Say, "I denounce _____ in Jesus name. My life belongs to God, and I am His property. Satan, you have no authority over me because I am under the ownership of God."

•Separate from any and all occult groups. The word "occult" means "hidden; clandestine." God doesn't want you to be a part of anything that opposes Him and that represents idols, evilness and wickedness. In fact, God doesn't want you to associate with people and groups that practice things "in the dark" according to Ephesians 5:6-13. Pray this prayer: "Jesus, open my spiritual eyes to the schemes of Satan, and to his deceptions so that I may walk in spiritual discernment and in the truth. Help me to know Your truth and walk in it."

•Develop in these areas and practice using these spiritual tools (weapons): discerning the voice of the Holy Spirit; declaring the Word of God (which releases God's angels); binding demons and declaring God's kingdom (His government) in a location/situation through prayer; "casting down" (exposing and challenging) ungodly thoughts (images, ideas) and arguments (logic, rationales) using the God's Word; operating in spiritual discernment and love; living by God's *rhema*; increasing in the anointing through fellowship with the Holy Spirit; fasting;

and praying in the spirit (tongues). Attend training classes and services at your church; or if they're not being offered at your church, find a ministry that is offering these trainings. Iron sharpens iron. Going around anointed atmospheres will help stir up the anointing and gifts of God in your own life, which He gives us to be witnesses for Him.

CHAPTER 6

A GIANT IN
MY STAIRWAY

*"David left his things with the keeper of supplies
and hurried out to the ranks to greet his brothers. As
he was talking with them, Goliath, the Philistine
champion from Gath, came out from the Philistine
ranks. Then David heard him shout his usual taunt
to the army of Israel."—1 Samuel 17:22-23 (NLT)*

HOW BOLD IS THE DEVIL? HE'LL SHOW-UP in
the most unlikely of places: the church; a
prayer meeting; he even showed-up once in
heaven while the angels of the Lord were presenting
themselves before the Heavenly Father during worship (Job 1:6). He was daring enough to show-up in
the wilderness while Jesus was fasting and praying
for forty days and forty nights. Satan even attempted
to deceive and mislead the Word (Logos) wrapped

in flesh (Jesus)...using the Word (logos)!! We sometimes forget just how bold our adversary can be. If Satan will throw Bible verses at God—twisting them out of context in order to deceive even Him—then I know he isn't scared to come in our churches, waltz right into our pulpits and do the same. Satan has no problem with coming into our churches, our homes, our lives—he'll take over them if we allow him to.

The Bible says the Philistine army traveled for several miles all the way from Philistia to the Valley of Elah in an attempt to push their way further into Judea where the Israelites were camped. The Israelite army and the Philistine army were at a stand-off there in the valley. The Philistines' solution was to pit their best fighter against their opposition's best fighter, as was customary in ancient times—the winner of the duel would secure a victory for their entire army, and the losing army would have to surrender their territory. This was a way of doing battle without spilling buckets of blood from thousands of men. Philistia's best fighter was Goliath, the champion of Gath, and Israel's best fighter was... Well, no one was daring and bold enough to step up to the plate; for this, Goliath mocked and made fun of the Israelites, blaspheming God Jehovah as a weak God commanding a pathetic army. He taunted God and the Israelites for days while waiting for a challenger. The longer this went on, the bolder Goliath grew.

Inaction does not guarantee peace and bring an end to conflict; actually, it does the opposite: it in-

tensifies the conflict by encouraging and embolden-
ing evil. Sitting back, doing nothing when someone
is mistreating you is not a method of bringing peace
into the situation. Thinking that a bully is going to
stop bullying you simply because you refuse to fight
back is a huge mistake. The bully will continue his or
her abuse until you fight back. Christians have been
deceived in this area. They've been told that fighting
back is against God's will. They've been made to believe self-defense and revenge seeking are the same
thing. Many church leaders have wrongly interpret-
ed the passage of Scripture in Matthew 5:39 where
Jesus told us to "resist not an evil person" (NLT), but
to instead turn the other cheek should one attack us;
but when one misunderstands Jesus' words they will
take them out of context and promote an attitude of
total inaction in the face of evil. The *Gill's Exposition
of the Entire Bible* sheds light on this passage. It says,

> "But I say unto you, that ye resist not evil,....
> This is not to be understood of any sort of
> evil, not of the evil of sin, of bad actions, and
> false doctrines, which are to be opposed; nor
> of the evil one, Satan, who is to be resisted;
> but of an evil man, an injurious one, who has
> done us an injury. We must not render evil
> for evil, or repay him in the same way; see
> James 5:6. Not but that a man may lawfully
> defend himself, and endeavor to secure him-
> self from injuries; and may appear to the civil

113

magistrate for redress of grievances; but he is
not to make use of private revenge."

As revealed in the commentary, there are some evils
that we are instructed in Scripture to resist. For
example, in 1 Corinthians chapter 5, Paul told the
Christians in Corinth to oppose immorality in their
church by kicking a man out of the church who was
sexually involved with his father's wife. In another
passage of Scripture, Jesus commended the Church
of Ephesus because of their resistance to false doctrines and false apostles (Revelation 2:2). In Romans
chapter 13, Paul explained the necessity of using the
sword to curtail evil and also frighten evil doers out
of acting on their evil schemes. In the gospels, Jesus violently whipped the moneychangers that were
exploiting the Temple worship for financial gain,
driving them out of the Temple in Jerusalem. In the
book of Hebrews, the eleventh chapter, which is aptly called "the hall of faith" (highlighting great men
and women of God who did extraordinary things as
a result of obeying God), there's a reference to those
who "became strong in battle and put whole armies
to flight" with swords and spears (vs. 34; NLT).

What was Jesus saying in Matthew chapter 5?
This was a parabolic message explaining the necessity of pursuing peace—it was common for Christ
to convey truths using idioms, which are a figurative language that is akin to slang. For example, in
Matthew 5:29, Jesus tells us to pluck out our eyes

and cut off our hands should they cause us to stumble into sin. But Jesus was not telling us to literally mutilate our bodies for the sake of righteousness; this was an idiom using an extreme example to convey a principle, that principle being that we should fear hell enough to not allow anything to cause us to stumble in our walk with God. Jesus, in Matthew 5:39, is using the same type of figurative language, expressing a principle using an idiom, letting us know we must be creative in our attempts to establish peace. Jesus furthermore reminds us that our physical bodies are only temporary; therefore, we're not to allow the wrongs done to our bodies to jeopardize our faith— and hence, jeopardize our eternal souls. Forgiveness is given in light of this fact—we are not forgiving for the sake of giving the other person a free pass, but for the sake of not becoming alienated from God's presence through un-forgiveness (Mark 11:25-26). As far as being able to defend oneself and one's family goes, that is a fundamental right afforded to all men by God. Just as in the Old Testament where there was a fundamental difference between murder and self-defense and involuntary manslaughter (Numbers 35:11-34), the same thing holds true today. Romans chapter 13 still upholds the death penalty for murder as ordained by God— His ministers "execute justice with the sword." Jesus advocated self-defense in Luke 22:36 when He told His disciples, "'But now,' he said, 'take your money and a traveler's bag. And if you don't have a sword, sell your cloak and buy one!'" (NLT).

Christians are supposed to resist evil, though not with evil intent (malice; revenge). Paul, in Ephesians 6:13, listed the armor that every Christian is supposed to wear. *Why wear armor?* Because we're in the middle of a war; because we're on a battlefield; because we're supposed to be fighting and *resisting* the principalities and powers that are running rampant in our world; and to sit back and passively do nothing is to encourage enemy forces and embolden them even more...as with Goliath. Because king Saul's men refused to face Goliath, Goliath felt comfortable blaspheming God in their presences. Goliath grew bolder, and bolder, and bolder day by day. People, today, are likewise becoming bolder as the church sits back and says nothing in the face of evil. It's a game of intimidation, and the church is losing due to its giving in to the hype.

In Ezekiel 22:30, God said, "And I sought for a man among them, that should make up the hedge, and stand in the gap before me for the land, that I should not destroy it: but I found none." What God was looking for were people who would stand in the gap through prayer and intercession and who would make up the hedge (a wall of protection) by teaching His people His standard of righteousness. He was calling for people who would pray and speak out against the evils in the land...so that He wouldn't have to pour out His wrath upon them. Being quiet and passive in the face evil only serves to help it advance and expedite our own destruction.

We all have an obligation to provide for and protect our households. As Christians, we are forbidden by God to force people to convert upon the threat of death and persecution. Christ instructs us as Believers to operate in love and gentleness, and Paul even explained in Romans 14:1 to be respectful of other people's opinions and beliefs even if they're wrong—don't try to argue them down and belittle them for what they think and believe. But when it comes to our own homes, we are allowed to establish the rules and hold others accountable to them. This is further emphasized in Paul's list of requirements for those seeking to be a bishop in 1 Timothy chapter three. There, Paul wrote, "He [a bishop of the church] must manage his own family well, having children who respect and obey him. For if a man cannot manage his own household, how can he take care of God's church?" (vs. 4-5; NLT).

I have learned the importance of praying over my family. I've had several instances where I almost lost my family members, and would have had it not been for my prayers covering them. I've had brushes with death myself that could have ended badly had it not been for the prayers of others covering me. I lost count of how many of these incidents I had—from a near fatal car crash, to a vicious street fight with a gang member in my neighborhood growing up as a child (I was 12 years old and he was 17 years old), to things I didn't even know about until years later...

like the time when I, being around 3 or 4 years old, drunk an entire cup of Ammonia when no one was looking...and lived. God had to show me that being a protector over my family was not a matter of owning a gun, but a matter of having a prayer life and covering them through prayer...as well as teaching my children how to pray. Job prayed every morning for his family; and due to his prayers, when Satan did try to attack his home, Satan couldn't because, as he complained to God, there was a hedge of protection all around Job's family, and he couldn't penetrate it (Job 1:10). But one particular night, I learned a very important lesson in spiritual warfare as it pertains to prayer, spiritual open doors, and protecting one's home from demonic intrusions.

THE BIG, THE BAD, THE UGLY

My daughter began having nightmares and couldn't sleep at night; my son was having them too. My kids would wake up quite often, complaining about seeing monsters. My daughter was a little more descriptive: she would see a big black creature with big red eyes in her dreams. It would tell her it was coming after her to get her—night after night this occurred. What was taking place in my home to allow such evil to grip my house? Well, it was during this time that I began to develop an addiction to internet pornography. Late in the midnight hours I would sit there with my laptop in my hands looking at porn. I didn't anticipate the backlash of such actions at the time. I thought I would be affected, but not my family—and in particularly, my kids. But, if there is one thing I know, it is this: Satan always seeks to destroy the children's lives more than anything else.

Listening to my kids wake-up in the middle of the night screaming, crying, and scared to be alone in their bedrooms reminded me of my experience as a child. My kids were now experiencing my nightmares; I knew it was real, it was demonic, but I couldn't quite put my finger on the root cause; I had a suspicion though: I figured my sinful actions may have played a role. But I didn't put it all together, not until...the night that my wife had a vision.

During this time, my kids were not the only ones having bad dreams. My wife would often wake up after a restless night and tell me about her dreams which usually entailed seeing snakes. My wife possesses a prophetic gift, and God deals very strongly with her in the area of dreams. Each time our house got robbed, she dreamed it before it happened. The Holy Spirit will show us things ahead of time so that we can start praying concerning those situations. We must seek God's wisdom regarding the matter, and in some cases, seek God for the wisdom to know if it is something to be rebuked—it may be demonically induced. But this was a repeat thing: the visions of snakes; the vision of a menacing entity described by my kids. It was one specific vision that did it for me: my wife woke up this time in the middle of the night, sweating profusely; her heart beating fast; her eyes stretched wide—I'd never seen her like that before. This time, what she described was more of a vision than a dream. She woke up claiming that she saw in a clear, vivid vision a humongous, black, hairy entity sitting in our stairway. My house was a two level, three bedroom house—the bedrooms were upstairs. My wife described an entity so large that it literally filled up the entire stairway...and it was only sitting. She was very detailed in her description. She said it was covered with black fur, and resonated a sense of menace and deep evil. It was in our house!!! How?! I knew how. I shared with her at that moment that I knew what was going on. I told my wife about my dabbling into pornography. I finally put it together: all of the visions and nightmares began during the same time that I started looking at pornography.

A powerful demon was tormenting my family due to my invitation to it through the sin of fornication (*porneia* in the Greek, from which the word "pornography" comes. *Porneia* means "sexual immorality"). I knew what I needed to do: kick it out! I let it in; I had to get rid of it. Immediately, I repented of the sin of fornication, and then I denounced that spirit. I started praying all over my house, anointing it with oil, decreeing that my house was no longer a territory open to and accepting of demonic spirits. I closed the doorway to the demonic; and afterwards, the nightmares ceased; my kids were now sleeping again; the atmosphere in my home was different.

When we discover the viciousness of sin and

discover the reality behind certain of our activities, that is enough to make us walk right out of the grip of sin. You don't need someone to lay hands on you and prophecy to you; you just need a dose of reality and a glimpse of what you're letting into your house through your actions. What demonic spirit are you bringing into your house? What will it bring with it when it comes: torment, sickness, murder, disease, more perversion, death? These are the things the Bible tells us demons bring—these are the things they brought me. From lust to suicidal thoughts, depression to confusion, at no time has an encounter with a demon benefited me and anyone one else around me.

THE SAME FAITH

As I just mentioned, there was a huge demon sitting in my stairway. According to the description of what my wife saw in a vision, it looked like Bigfoot sitting in my stairway; but not all demons are big; there are some demons that are much smaller in size, literally. People who've been given the unfortunate opportunity to see spirits/demons (such as Bill Weise, who wrote about his experience in his book *23 Minutes in Hell*, and Robin Harfouche, the New Age priestess who was being groomed by Shirley McLaine before she converted to Christianity—Robin was given the ability to see in the spirit by her grandmother, who was a powerful witch; and as a child, she'd see spirits), not all spirits are the same size. Clarita, who we talked about in chapter three, saw a big demon and a small one attacking her. Some demons are more territorial than others. Some demons and fallen angels have more authority and power than others, as is revealed in Daniel chapter 10 (here is the incident where the archangel Gabriel, while on his way to deliver a message to Daniel, was intercepted by a fallen angel that was so powerful that Gabriel needed the archangel Michael to help him break through its defenses. This fallen angel was a high ranking one that reigned over the Persian Empire). That is why Jesus said regarding some demons, "...this kind goeth not out but by prayer and fasting" (Matthew 17:21). The fasting and prayer is so that there will be less of you in the way, not so that there will be more of God at your disposal. The name of Jesus possesses enough authority to make any demon flee, but some demons are bold enough to try you just to see if you sincerely believe in the authority of the name of Jesus (Acts 19:11-20). This is why you have to crucify your flesh before you go up against certain demons.

The same name that brings us salvation is the same name that brings us deliverance. The same faith you used to believe unto salvation is the same faith you need to believe for a healing. The same faith it takes to slay big demons is the same faith that slays small ones. Whether it be cancer or a small pain in the foot, finances or family problems, the only thing you need to do is *believe*...on the name of Jesus and claim His promises. Just believe in what God said.

CHAPTER 6 OBJECTIVES:

•Ask God today for the wisdom to confront evil in love. Don't ignore and condone wrongdoing, but don't render "evil for evil" either (Romans 12).

•Pray over your family today. Get some anointed oil (prayed over by your pastor who is anointed or by an anointed minister) and anoint each family member with it while saying, "I cover you with the blood of Jesus and pray God's protection over you this day. No weapon against us shall prosper today. Guide our steps today, Jesus. It is in Your name I pray, Amen."

•Pray over your household, work-space, etc. with that same oil (if at work, do so before others arrive so as not to cause confusion or alarm). Anoint your desk, cubicle, classroom, etc. and say, "I declare in the name of Jesus that no demonic spirit may enter and operate in this place. I bind every evil spirit today and ask that the angels of the Lord occupy this space. Holy Spirit, I consecrate this space to You so that You may reign in here, in Jesus name, Amen."

•If you or your loved-ones are having nightmares and bad dreams, then first check to see what is being played on the television, radio, etc. (this goes back to our objectives from chapter 3). Afterwards, anoint them or yourself and say, "I thank You Lord that this mind and body belongs to You. We/I denounce Satan and plead the blood of Jesus over this mind. I rebuke the spirit of fear in Jesus name."

One Giant Away

TALKING TRASH

*"And the Philistine said unto David, Am I a dog,
that thou comest to me with staves? And the Philistine
cursed David by his gods. And the Philistine said to
David, Come to me, and I will give thy flesh unto the
fowls of the air, and to the beasts of the field."*
—*1Samuel 17:43-44*

O YOU RECALL FROM OUR PREVIOUS chapter how I talked about Goliath's infiltration into the Israelite's yard with all of his blasphemies and threats against God Jehovah and the Israelites? I need to expound on something that's a critical issue when it comes to faith, life, victory, and even defeat: the power of words. This can't be overemphasized or overstated. Words are powerful; they are life-changers; they are world-shapers; they build up and they tear down; and as you'll see, words are Satan's main tool which he uses against us all.

The Bible repeatedly stresses to us the importance of watching what we say. Jesus said we must all answer to God in judgment for every word spoken in secret (Matthew 12:36). Solomon said the power of life and death is in our tongues (Proverbs 18:21). Solomon also said harsh words are like swords, and a wise man's tongue brings healing (Proverbs 12:18). James 1:26 explains that the man that cannot control his tongue, his religion is useless. James also tells us that our tongues can set a person's life on a certain course, and that if we mislead people doctrinally we will face the greater condemnation (3:1-12).

We are not to waste words—including God's Word. In Matthew 7:6, Jesus said we are not to give pearls (God's revelations) to swine (individuals who don't want to know the truth). We need to be Spirit led in our witnessing, and don't try to ram the truth down a person's throat when they express a lack of interest in the truth. When the Bible tells us that the harvest is ripe in Luke 10:2, it is saying that there are people who are ready and willing to hear the gospel right now and the Holy Spirit is eager to lead us to those hungry souls. Sadly, the laborers (Christians who're willing to witness) are few, although witnessing is Christ's commission given to all Believers.

THE FIGHT BEFORE THE FIGHT

While the Israelites were nestled in their encampment looking over at the opposing army across from them in the Valley of Elah, the massive Goliath suddenly emerged from the enemy's camp and started taunting them. Goliath first threw out a challenge to any man in the Israelite camp to step to him, then he began to taunt the God of Israel. He grew bolder and bolder with his insults and more blasphemous as time progressed. Realize: Goliath didn't emerged from the enemy's camp and charge straight at the Israelites like a bull with his sword drawn; he, instead, hammered the Israelites with insult after insult. He was trash-talking the people of God in an attempt to get into their heads and break their spirits.

It's normal to talk trash to your competition in a sporting event. Doing this gets you pumped up; it gets the adrenaline flowing. Most times, when a person dishes out trash talk it's because they are trying to amp themselves up. It's a psychological tactic used to give one an edge in the fight. They know that if they can intimidate their opponent(s) before their match and get into their head(s) they will have already won the match. When two fighters are about to compete, they'll engage in a stare-down followed by trash talk for the purpose of making their opponent think they are badder, meaner, and more powerful than they actually are. Many of Mike Tyson's fights were won just during the stare-down: his opponents quivering in fear before the first punch was thrown; many of them punched-out by the hype before entering the ring. Yes, Tyson was mean; he was a heavy hitter; *but Buster Douglas wasn't intimidated.* There was the story of one of Tyson's opponents, Michael

Spinks, whose manager went to Tyson's locker room right before their fight; when he arrived in the room, he witnessed Tyson punching holes in the wall. This so frightened Spinks' manager that he went back to his fighter's (Spinks) room and unknowingly transfered his fear onto his fighter. Spinks lost terribly in the ring, but the fight was really lost the moment his manager lost faith in his ability to slay the beast (Tyson) in that locker room. The devil wants us to lose faith in God before we even set out to do what God says do. Satan wants to get into our heads before we step onto the field. Satan wants our giants to defeat us in the stare-down so that we will end up backing out of the fight; so that we'll give up before we even attempt to step out in obedience to God by faith.

Before Satan can get into our heads, he seeks to get into our spirits. Satan's goal is to infect our spirits so that our spirits will produce toxic thoughts in our heads. The spirit behind the words reveals the true nature and intent of the words. It's not necessarily *what* is said that we have to pay attention to, but *why* it is said. People sometimes complement us for the purpose of manipulating us. People sometimes insult us for the purpose of motivating us (this hardly works). Some people will quote Bible verses in an attempt to sway listeners to their side, but their real goal is to sway the listeners away from God. Remember how Satan repeatedly stated "It is written" in at attempt to deceive Jesus in the desert? He was telling the truth about what was written in the Scriptures, but he was being deceptive in why he was quoting the Scriptures: he was deliberately taking them out of context and twisting their meanings around in an attempt to trick Jesus out of fulfilling His ultimate mission, which was to die on the cross for our sins. Satan is a liar, and even when he quotes the Bible he does so with the intention to ultimately mislead us. Satan's messages may contain 90% truth and 10% error, just enough "leaven" (false doctrine) to contaminate the rest of the 90%. Throughout history men have twisted Bible verses and quoted them out of context just enough to defend racism, slavery, murder, genocide, idolatry, and even sexual perversions. Your spirit determines your worldview, and your worldview determines your nature, intent, and fruit behind your words.

Joshua and Caleb didn't just have a different perspective from the rest of the Israelite camp while in the wilderness, they had a different spirit. Proverbs 20:27 tells us the spirit of a man is the Lord's candlestick, which He uses to search out a person's heart. The New Living Translation translates it this way: "The LORD's light penetrates the human spirit, exposing every hidden motive." Allowing the Holy Spirit to speak to our spirits is the key to discerning the spirit behind other people's words. That is why John, in 1 John 4:1, tells us not to believe every spirit but test the spirit of every preacher, teacher, prophet and speaker to see if they're led by the Holy Spirit or the spirit of the antichrist. He said the spirit of the antichrist has a particular worldview: it incorrectly views Christ Jesus as a metaphor, a symbol for some type of cosmic consciousness, a bodiless mass waiting to grip or possess men. This is the view of Jesus held by all New Agers, Hindus, Buddhists and many other cult groups...including the Freemasons, who see Christ as a carrier of a special knowledge (light) that all men should obtain for their own apotheosis (transformation into godhood). They don't see Jesus as the savior of mankind, as one to be worshiped solely and exclusively; but rather, as one among several "enlightened" beings who discovered this secret knowledge and became powerful. The spirit of the antichrist, plain and simple, views Jesus outside of the lens of the Bible, and therefore misunderstands and misrepresents Him. The Holy Spirit, on the other hand, reveals to us the true nature and identity of Jesus the Christ, confirming in our hearts that Jesus is truly the Christ and that He actually did come down from heaven and dwell among men in human flesh; that He did die on the cross and rise from the grave on the third day. The spirit of antichrist views Christ as an impostor, as one who evaded the cross. This is the teaching promoted by Islam: that Jesus' body was swapped with an imposter's on the cross, so He never died, and hence, never rose from the grave. This is why you can't reconcile and mix Christianity with any other religion: the spirit driving Christianity (Holy Spirit) conflicts with the spirit of the world (Ephesians 2:1-2). Jesus said

the world will always misunderstand and misinter-
pret His words because the world (those who don't
have a relationship with Jesus) doesn't have the Holy
Spirit (John 14:17). The correct perspective of Jesus
comes from the Holy Spirit, not philosophy and human reasoning or an institution of higher learning.

When men have the Holy Spirit in them, it is
impossible for them to truly accept and support sin
and wickedness. Their consciences will be grieved
by such things. This is why 1 John 3:9 says whoever
is born of God sins not. John also said in 1 John 2:20
that we have an "unction" (*chrisma* in the Greek,
meaning "anything smeared on; an ointment") from
God and we know "all things"—in other words, we,
as Christians, have an anointing from God to know
the truth when we hear it; we have the Holy Spirit in
us to help us discern when what we're hearing isn't
quite right. The Holy Spirit reminds us of the words
of Jesus and helps us to operate with the "mind of
Christ" (John 14:16-17, 26; 1 Corinthians 2:16). The
mind of Christ refers to the heart and intent of God
in relation to His Word. It is possible for a Believer to
ignore the Holy Spirit and listen to the wrong voice
in their heads (the wrong spirit, the wrong teaching
and doctrine) and end-up fighting against the Holy
Spirit in their lives. This is why Paul said we should
not "quench" the Holy Spirit in 1 Thessalonians 5:9.
The word "quench" in the Greek means "to extin-
guish; to stifle, suppress"—therefore, don't suppress
the Holy Spirit in your life. Don't smother Him and

ignore Him; and furthermore, don't replace Him in your life and attempt to convince yourself of lies.

Goliath was intimidating indeed: he was as big of a threat as he presented himself; he truly was capable of crushing a man's head with a single hand; he was a big deal and someone to fear; he had an intimidating stare that could pierce armor. During the stare-down Goliath punked every man in the Israelite army, *but David wasn't impressed*. David saw himself as a bigger deal because he realized the God he served could thump Goliath away like a bug. Goliath's stare didn't work on David, and this is why David didn't back down. David didn't listen to the hype surrounding Goliath; he talked about the hype surrounding God. The Holy Spirit will rise up on the inside of us during times of great difficulty and challenges and cause God's anointing to overtake us, therefore causing us to operate in a divine boldness and with an extraordinary ability that's beyond our natural capabilities. This is what's known as *the gift of faith*. This was the result of the Holy Spirit inside of David. The Holy Spirit causes us to take on a right perspective concerning our problems and to walk in a divine revelation in the midst of our circumstances; and we consequently talk divine trash in the face of the biggest devils. Just listen to little David's trash talk in the face of a nearly 10ft tall, 800+lbs monster:

"...for who is this uncircumcised Philistine, that he should defy the armies of the living

God? [Translated: "Who does this fool think he is defying my God?] . . . . The LORD that delivered me out of the paw of the lion, and out of the paw of the bear, he will deliver me out of the hand of this Philistine [Translated: "I ain't worried about this fool. He gonna' fall like the rest of them]. . . . Thou comest to me with a sword, and with a spear, and with a shield: but I come to thee in the name of the LORD of hosts, the God of the armies of Israel, whom thou hast defied. This day will the LORD deliver thee into mine hand; and I will smite thee, and take thine head from thee; and I will give the carcases of the host of the Philistines this day unto the fowls of the air, and to the wild beasts of the earth; that all the earth may know that there is a God in Israel. And all this assembly shall know that the LORD saveth not with sword and spear: for the battle is the LORD'S, and he will give you into our hands [Translated: "You messed with the wrong God, and now you about to pay]" (1 Samuel 17:26, 37, 45-47).

Anointed Christians (not religious folks who reject the presence and power of the Holy Spirit) don't just face demons, they talk trash in the face of demons. Spirit-filled Christians don't just tell the devil to get lost, they tell the devil to get lost **or else...** You can talk trash to the devil, to demons, to giants, to trials and tribulations, to death and to temptation because you are anointed to win this fight. You are anointed to talk trash in the face of the enemy. You talk trash by reminding the giants in your way of the size of your God. Here's some *anointed trash talk*:

1. When sickness grips your body and whispers in your ear that you'll never get free, remind sickness that Jesus whipped its behind on the cross when He took our stripes upon His back...and then began to speak God's healing promises over your body daily.

2. When death tries to frighten you as a Christian and make you think this is the end, remind death that Jesus snatched its teeth out on the cross when He rose from the grave—then ask death to let you see its dentures. Rub it in.

3. When Satan reminds you of your past, ask him if he has his swimming trunks ready...because he's getting ready to get tossed into a *certain lake*.

Oh, and don't forget to remind him that all things work together for your good. So, let them tell your story and talk about your past; that's just evidence that God can change and transform anyone.

4. When fear tells you that you're going to fail, begin to remind fear of the promises of God spoken over your life and in His Word. Speak those promises out loud and watch fear's knees begin to buckle.

5. When bills tell you they're getting ready to crush you, remind them that you serve a God who is rich in blessings and able to do above and beyond what you can even ask or imagine. If you are a tither and a giver, you have a right to talk trash to financial difficulty, and remind it that your God is going to meet all of your needs according to His riches in glory.

MAKING GRASSHOPPERS OUT OF MEN

Don't let the devil in your head. Don't internalize his words, accusations and threats. He'll keep hammering you with his words while attempting to wear you down, but don't give-in. Just remember who you are really dealing with: a slew-footed, fork-tongued liar. The name "Satan" means "accuser." He's good at accusing you in your mind every time you slip-up and make a mistake, every time you have a bad thought, and whenever you try to move forward in life. Satan reminds us of our mistakes, failures, weaknesses, and shortcomings. Satan knows that if he can simply repeat something enough times—repeat lies in our ears—we may start to believe them; so he'll keep reminding us of our failures, weaknesses, shortcomings, mistakes, etc. He'll keep saying things like:

You're a failure. You messed-up. You won't succeed. You failed last time. You're a nobody. You're not good enough, smart enough, pretty enough, educated enough, popular enough.

You're the black sheep of the family. Nobody likes you. People only tolerate you; they don't really want you around. You'd be better off dead. You're a waste of space. Nothing you've come up with works. You're a problem. You have a problem. You're just an angry man. You're just an insecure woman. You're a drama queen. You're lazy, sorry, and stupid. You need to be on medication. You will never get a job. Let's face it: have you ever accomplished anything good in your life? You're just a crackhead drug addict. You're an addict. You will never get free from this. Ah ha! You thought you were free, didn't you? But you relapsed. Look at you now! I told you you'll never shake the habit. You're the child no one wanted. You are a mistake. A hundred people attempted to do that, and none of them succeeded; so what makes you think you'll succeed?

As a man thinks in his heart, so is he (Proverbs 23:7). When someone constantly tells you that you're a big clumsy, lazy, no good problem; you're a basket case and nobody wants or likes you; or they constantly remind you of your mistakes, failures, and criticize you constantly and never seek to find anything good about you, you may begin to act accordingly. You can shape a person's life by speaking words over them that will shape their thinking and perceptions of themselves and of the world around them.

Married couples tend to fall apart due to the words shared in the relationship. Trust is destroyed due to negative criticism—when criticism is given, but it isn't preceded or proceeded by praise. For every criticism there needs to be at least several praises; but sadly, in most marriages, people who have begun to lose respect and love for one another develop resentment towards each other and seek only to criticize, criticize, criticize, belittle, demean, insult, and blame each other; when this happens, the marriage is on the fast track to divorce. Some wives are guilty of this, which is why the Bible says in Proverbs 14:1, "A wise woman builds her home, but a foolish woman tears it down with her own hands" (NLT). And in Proverbs 21:9, Solomon said, "It's better to live alone in the corner of an attic than with a quarrelsome wife in a lovely home" (NLT). Many women, being more emotional than men and desiring communication over sex (the man's biggest need next to respect), can tend to pinpoint every mistake the man makes and talk him down till the point that he shuts down emotionally and loses trust in her. This is why Paul told fathers, in Ephesians 6:4, not to push their children to the point of exasperation and anger. This is done by constantly criticizing and burdening them with the pressures and expectations of perfection. It is problematic to expect others to do what we ourselves could not—and cannot—do; and yet, this is how families are broken-up. Concerning husbands, Paul told them to wash their wives with the Word of

God, which means to teach them the Word. Rather than doing this, some men talk down to their wives, making them feel insecure. Rather than doing what Peter instructed us to do in 1 Peter 3:7 and honoring our wives, treating them with understanding (as to their emotions and nature), and confirming to them that they are partners, not servants; some men treat them as doormats and make them feel as if they're not included in their lives. Peter instructed wives to likewise wear the "beauty of a gentle and quiet spirit, which is so precious to God," and to honor their husbands as Sarah did by esteeming him even to the point of reverencing him, not talking him down (vs. 4-6). Everything about building a house is based on the principle of speaking the right words in the right manner at the right time. This takes God's wisdom.

Praise builds people's confidence and self-esteem. Praise makes people believe they're accepted and cherished. A father doesn't want a necktie for his birthday or for father's day; he simply wants the respect of his wife and children. He wants his wife to build him up, especially if he has to leave his home morning after morning and get beaten down by his boss, by a society that doesn't understand him, and by people looking to tear him down and make him feel low. The praises of his wife causes the stress of the day to melt away. Knowing that she believes in him and also hearing her tell him that she believes in him is enough to make him get up the next day and face the world with a fierce confidence. Knowing that he doesn't have to earn his wife's respect, and that he's not being punished for not living up to all of her expectations, is all the fuel he needs to make it in a cruel world. Praise builds up children and wives in the same way. Letting your wife know that your love and devotion isn't something she has to earn is enough to provide an unparalleled sense of security inside her heart. Praise and affirmation does wonders for people; it has the uncanny ability to take broken people and transform their lives.

Satan is trying to produce human grasshoppers. He wants them hopping around in churches, homes, society, etc. We must recognize what he is trying to do to us. He wants to make us feel small. Talk trash to that grasshopper mentality! *Talk some!*

The Bible says, "So get rid of all the filth and evil in your lives, and humbly accept the Word God as planted in your hearts, for it has the power to save your souls. But don't just listen to God's Word. You must do what it says. Otherwise, you are only fooling yourselves" (James 1:21, NLT). So, stop living as if you are hopeless, because you are not. People give-in to sin and destruction because they feel frustrated, but realize that God has a plan and a reward set aside for us if we do His will. God hasn't given up on you—He never will. But while there's still time to get it right, do so. Quit fighting against the truth, humble yourself and accept the fact that God does love you and desire to use you. Quit the pity party and start praising God for what He's about to do in your life. Talk trash to the spirit of heaviness! Talk trash to that depression! Stop fooling yourself by convincing yourself that the liar (Satan) is telling the truth about you. Stop it! Stop repeating what the devil says to you and about you, and start repeating what God says to you and about you.

FORGIVENESS: THE KEY TO EMPTYING OUT THE TRASH

Cellular Biologists have made an astounding discovery: they have discovered that cells contain memories. For example, there is the case of an eight year old girl who received a heart transplant from a ten year old girl who was viciously murdered by an intruder one night. Soon after the transplant, the girl began having violent nightmares about her donor's murder. The nightmares were reoccurring. The girl could see the killer's face clearly in her dreams. Her mother finally took her to a psychiatrist, who found nothing abnormal about the girl, and then she took her to the police. The girl revealed to the authorities gruesome details about the murder, which matched the evidence the authorities had. The girl reported that she knew who the murderer was, which led to the arrest of the man who murdered the donor. According to her psychiatrist, "the time, the weapon, the place, the clothes he wore, what the little girl he killed had said to him . . . everything the little heart transplant recipient reported was completely accurate" (*Cellular Memory In Organ Transplants*, www.effective-mind-control.com). There are other cases in which people who've received organ transplants have experienced sudden desires and changes in personality—these changes being consistent with the donor's personality. As the evidence reveals, there are more things going on in our bodies than what science previously understood. When a person suffers a trauma, a devastating loss, a deep heartbreak, a pain, a happy moment, an excitement, etc., these experiences and traumas (data) are then stored in the person's cells. Memories don't just go away. Hurt and pain doesn't simply disappear. Trauma can't be wiped away with a hand gesture. We may try to suppress memories of things done to us, but suppression is not the same as healing; actually, it is a form of self-deception and denial: things that prevent healing. God never asked you to be Superman or Super-girl and miraculously erase that which you can't erase. God never asked you to forget what was said or done to you. You can't! He did, however, tell you to get the memories of the things done and said to you and bring them to the forefront of your mind on purpose. Why? Because when you forgive, you must be conscious of what you're letting go of; you must be conscious of what you're releasing. Forgiveness isn't forgetting; it's an act of consciously choosing to release a debt owed to you by another for the purpose of aligning or realigning yourself with God so that He can continue the work He began in you.

Forgiveness opens the door of your soul and allows the Holy Spirit to enter into your body and bring healing into every fiber of your being. Healing is defined as "the process of restoring, setting right, repairing." Forgiveness begins this process. Forgiveness is when you choose to relinquish control of the situation to God, then the healing occurs as God begins to restore and repair your soul by helping you to understand why you went through the things you did; and not only will God give you understanding, but He will affirm or reaffirm who you are in Christ. A big part of the healing process is the rediscovery of your identity in Christ through God's Word and the gaining of a new perspective on life by developing a biblical worldview. The devil used words to tear you down, and now God is using words to build you up. As Proverbs 16:24 declares: "Gracious words are like a honeycomb, sweetness to the soul and health to the body." Perceiving things through God's eye-view erases a lot of confusion and helps you to understand not only where the real blame lies, but also what the real solution is (2 Chronicles 7:14). Healing comes through spiritual growth and maturity in the understanding of the Word, and not through time. You will finally stop blaming yourself for the rape, abuse, or trauma you experienced, and start realizing the spiritual (the particularly demonic) elements behind the things you've experienced; you will then begin to attack the real enemy, Satan, and also take responsibility for your own actions as you move forward in your life. God will reveal to you the things you must take responsibility for, and the things you simply need to take authority over in prayer. God will give you His joy and peace through His Spirit. Lastly, God will penetrate every cell and fiber of your being and free you from the iniquitous roots established in your bloodline through your ancestry. This is what it means to *be made whole* (John 5:6). Forgive daily.

CHAPTER 7 OBJECTIVES:

•Read all of the Bible verses concerning the promises of God for His people.

•Meditate only on God's Word today, not on your problems or ungodly things.

•Speak the promises of God over your life and circumstances out loud, all day today.

•Use the trash-talk already expressed in this chapter when fear, worry and sorrow strikes.

•Say something good to someone you know today. Practice making the complementing and edification of others a regular habit of yours. Find something good about them to comment on rather than looking for something wrong or bad about them to talk about—including yourself.

•Forgive others today, including yourself, for any wrongs done to you. Remember to empty out the emotional, spiritual and mental trash daily through forgiveness.

CHAPTER 8

Did You Forget About The Other Ones?

"And he took his staff in his hand, and chose him five smooth stones out of the brook, and put them in a shepherd's bag which he had, even in a scrip; and his sling was in his hand: and he drew near to the Philistine."—1 Samuel 17:40

GOD GIVES US THE WEAPONS TO USE to defeat the challenges facing us in our places of dominion. As long as we are where we belong in life, His anointing will remain on our lives; and as long as we're anointed, giants are no match for us. It only took one stone from David's sling to knock out Goliath, allowing David to decapitate him with his own sword. That stone was anointed. If God gives you a dream, don't worry about whether or not others have failed at accomplishing that same dream or others are copying after you or attempting to beat you to the punch because you're especially anointed to succeed. Don't worry about what others are doing or what they have that you don't have; focus on what God has given you. If it's a business, focus on that. If it's a certain gift, focus on that. If it's a certain mantle or anointing (in the Bible there are many different types of spiritual gifts and anointings), then simply use it and stop comparing yourself to others. We are not all designed to accomplish the same tasks, have the same dreams and goals, and act the same. We're uniquely created by God. The fruit of all that we do as Believers is designed to bring glory to God and to lead men to Christ; however, what we do differs. So many people toss away their anointed stone because they see others carrying swords, shields, and spears. They think they're inadequate because their weapon isn't the same as someone else's; and yet, God is the master of using unconventional things to accomplish impossible His will. When God proves a point, He does it creatively. Paul told us God uses the foolish things to embarrass those who believe they are wise (1 Corinthians 1:27). God enjoys humiliating people who are filled with pride and think they are better than others because of what they possess. God hates pride. God hates an arrogant look. When people begin to act like they don't need God because they have their money, degrees, guns, bombs, and allies, God has a way of turning the tables on them.

It only took a handful of terrorists to humble the greatest nation with the most dominate military in the world today (America) during the 9/11 terrorist attacks. But, at least America was humbled by men; Egypt, on the other hand, was reduced to rubble by a series of plagues consisting of frogs, locust, blood and darkness. God used the elements of nature to humble the man (Pharaoh) who believed he was the reincarnation of the Egyptian sun god, Ra, on earth and reduce the world's superpower during that time to nothingness. People who arrogantly assume that they don't need God because they have everything that they need to make it on their own find themselves being humbled by job losses, economic crashes, the inability to find a job despite having a degree, family tragedies despite all of the safety measures they've taken to prevent it, etc.; and according to Bible prophecy, things are going to get worse for those who put their trust in money. James 5:1-3 explains that there is coming a day when all of the gold and silver that men have been hoarding to protect themselves will suddenly and instantly become worthless. Yes, a great worldwide economic collapse leading to a shift in lifestyles globally is prophesied to come. In Jeremiah chapter seventeen, God promised protection and blessings only to those who put their hope and trust in Him.

God uses unconventional weapons. He gives us unconventional weapons. What you need in order to accomplish God's will for your life is already in your possession. God built you with a purpose in mind; and when God built you, He endowed you in order that you might complete His intended task for your life. The problem is that through time we often become enshrouded by so many extra layers of identities God didn't intend for us. Layers of man-made identities are placed on us. Layers of people's expectations, hopes and dreams are placed on us (even by parents who want their children to live their dreams rather than follow God's plans for them), and layers of problems, misconceptions, erroneous doctrines, stinking thinking and emotional baggage are placed on us. Discovering one's true identity, gifts and purpose entails God having to peel away the many layers hiding the *treasure* He has placed in our *vessels* (bodies) so that the truth is revealed; so, stop looking for others to shape you and start spending time in the presence of God so that He can strip you of everything that is hindering you from becoming the you that He intended for you to be and accomplishing the task that He intended for you to accomplish.

What layers have been placed on you, hiding your potential greatness? What words were spoken over your life causing you to develop complexes and layers of false identities that impeded your progress and ambitions in life? Well, we talk about individuals who managed to strip away layers (words, labels and identities placed on them) and become great in life: Albert Einstein had to strip away the label that was placed on him by one of his earlier school teachers when they called him "an unteachable fool". And even Oprah Winfrey stripped away the label given to her by her boss who called her "unfit for television" just before demoting her. Walt Disney had to strip away the label placed on him by his boss who told him that he lacked any good ideas. Michael Jordan had to strip away the label placed on him due to his being cut from his high school basketball team— the label being given to him was that he wasn't good enough to play basketball. Thomas Edison, one of the greatest and most celebrated inventors in the world, had a big label placed on him when he was a child in school: he was sent home from school one day with a note from his school teacher addressed to his parents that read: Thomas Edison is "too stupid to learn" and stated that he needed to be removed from school. Edison's mother began homeschooling him instead, helping to peel back the layers of harsh criticism placed on him by his teacher...who probably didn't know that Edison was partially deaf. A Black woman named Biddy Mason, who was born into slavery on August 15, 1818, was swamped with labels: she was told she was a slave, property, inferior, unintelligent, etc.; and yet, this woman won her freedom and went on to become one of the nation's leading and wealthiest real estate tycoons; she even built the first Black church in California.

Now, these people were able to do extraordinary things after peeling off all of the *"you can't"* and *"that's never been done before"* and *"you're too stu-*

149

pid and *"you're not cut out for this"* labels placed on them. If they could do this with the help of others or even on their own and manage to expose talents and abilities inside of them that changed the world, then what do you think you can do with the help of God? Furthermore, what do you think God can bring out of you—or place in you—if you surrender totally to Him? The Bible says, "The secret things belong to God" in Deuteronomy 29:29, but God is willing to share them with those who love Him and obey His Commandments. Forget what "they" said about you and find out what God says about you, and what He can do in and through you if you yield to Him. Be just like David, who didn't allow his brothers' labels of "you're too small" and "you don't belong here" to stop him from slaying the giant they were too afraid to face and being elevated to a superior status than them (as king). Speak to yourself. Say, "I am a king/queen." Say, "I am the head and not the tail, above and not beneath, the lender and not the borrower, victorious and not defeated, an overcomer and not an underachiever, wealthy and not poor, healed and not sick, delivered and not bound." Say, "I am blessed and highly favored, and I am not a slave to sin; but I am a slave to righteousness." Do as the Bible instructs us to do and "put on" the new man (label) which is modeled after Christ Jesus (Ephesian 4:24).

PREPARING FOR THE UNEXPECTED

David didn't just grab one stone when facing Goliath; he grabbed five stones. Some people speculate that he grabbed extra stones just in case the first shot missed or didn't quite slow the monstrous assailant down, but others believe that David grabbed the extra stones because he was aware of the fact that Goliath had several friends. There were several other giants who are also listed in Scripture besides Goliath, which David and his men came across: Ishbi-benob (2 Samuel 21:16-17); Saph (2 Samuel 21:18); Lahmi, the brother of Goliath (1 Chronicles 20:5); and also "a man of great stature, whose fingers and toes were four and twenty, six on each hand, and six on each foot" (1 Chronicles 20:7). Whether or not David was counting on facing these other giants during his confrontation with Goliath is unknown—and probably unlikely. But whatever the case, David was wise enough to prepare for the unexpected.

If God promises you a blessing you should know by now that it (the blessing) will come with a giant—in fact, the presence of a giant is an indication that you are in the right location. Giants are demonic oppositions to your calling. But just because you slew one giant, that doesn't mean that you now have the right to let your guard down and relax. There are others waiting. In fact, one giant, Ishbi-benob, would've killed David in a later confrontation had it not been for Abishai, one of David's men who came to his rescue and saved him by killing the giant. This is why God wants to connect us with other men and women of faith, other giant killers: because there are times when you will need others to intercede for you and fight with you to defeat certain giants. There are times when we grow weak and need others to watch our backs. God places people of faith in our lives to help us accomplish the tasks He has for us. Nothing God purposes for your life can be accomplished by you alone. Get the lone ranger idea out of your head. If you're anything like me, then you've looked at one too many Hollywood action movies where a single person (Chuck Norris, Steven Seagal, Arnold Schwarzenegger, etc.) will single-handedly dismantle an entire army of assailants using CQC or some other martial art with their bare hands, but in real life there are no directors present to yell "Cut" when you don't get the upper hand. This isn't a movie; it's reality; and in reality, you only get one shot at it. Don't take chances and stay isolated. Don't retreat into a corner and think that you can make it without the help of other Believers. Don't even count on defeating the battle within yourself alone. Keep a few trustworthy accountability partners around you. In Hebrews 10:25, God reveals to us that by remaining around the saints (those who are spiritually mature) we are able to maintain our right focus; for, by being around the saints we position ourselves around men and women who will "exhort" (*parakaleō* in Greek, meaning "to console, encourage, and strengthen by consolation; to comfort") us in the faith. When the spirit/giant of heaviness tries to attack you with depression, you need a fellow giant-slayer nearby who can stick a Holy Ghost javelin through that demon's heart and then pull you back to your feet. When that spirit/giant of lust tries to pull you back into that pit of perversion (porn, strip clubs, promiscuity, prostitution, homosexuality, etc.), you need a fellow giant killer who's spiritually mature to help you, not judge you; to help you remain focused while praying away the spiritual influence trying to send you back to *the old ways*. When you are marching into your Promised Land, you need an army of giant-slayers to help you take the land for the Kingdom of God. It takes an army of prayer warriors and worshipers to take back nations from the hands of the enemy. The devil relies on an army of demons to do big things; God likewise calls together an army of like-minded saints to do big things. Anything big (and God's plans for you are BIG) takes an army to accomplish. Let God position the right people around the vision He has given you; and then, after God has assembled your team, do as Habakkuk 2:2 says and "write down the vision" and keep your team focused on it so that nobody will become distracted or misdirected.

Satan's attacks against us are continuous. Just because we survived one attack, that doesn't mean the fight is over. It's never over. It won't be over until we die. You start the business, and now your family is experiencing turmoil: your daughter got pregnant by a horny boy, or your son just joined a gang. *Here we go again!* It's another fight. You just climbed out of the pit of financial ruin and reached a place of financial stability and wealth...and now a doctor has just diagnosed you with cancer. The warfare against you never ends. You break free from a drug addiction, but then you find yourself facing charges from something ten years ago that you forgot about...and now the courtroom drama is starting all over again. The fight never ends. You finally get the job and now the company is closing. You finally start your ministry, but now sickness grips your body, siphoning off money out of your bank account. You finally begin the building project and then an inspector gives you bad news about the land you're building on or slaps you with a slew of code violations that bring your project to a complete halt—or unexpected expenses arise and you run out of money to complete the project. You purchase your dream home, but afterwards discover that it's falling apart and will need a ton of repairs you just don't have the money for at the moment. You made your first million...and now you're being sued. The old adage goes as such: If it ain't one thing, it's another. Life is difficult and unpredictable enough on its own, but when demonic spirits jump into the mix with their constant schemes and plots to derail and destroy you, the problem only intensifies. That's why we must learn to follow...

AN UNPREDICTABLE, SPONTANEOUS GOD

Solomon wrote, "Just as you cannot understand the path of the wind or the mystery of a tiny baby growing in its mother's womb, so you cannot understand the activity of God, who does all things" (Ecclesiastes 11:5, NLT). Many Christians are frustrated over the fact that they know God plans to bless them, but they don't know how He's going to bless them. Many have already mapped out their lives, only to assume that God has abandoned them when their plans are derailed. That's a misconception. God doesn't exist to serve our will; we exist to serve His. God doesn't exist to fulfill our dreams; we exist to fulfill His; and He isn't supposed to follow us; we're supposed to follow Him. But following God takes consistency and the willingness to do things we've never done before and go places we've never gone before. God may tell you to do things one way in one situation, and then tell you to do something totally different in another situation. David used a slingshot to kill Goliath, but he didn't use a slingshot when fighting the Philistine army. God may give you another method when dealing with a different challenge. One of the mistakes Christians make when it comes to God is they quickly assume that they don't have to continue in prayer after receiving a blessing. Some believe that they have "arrived". Many don't realize or forget that some blessings and movements are seasonal. Something may have been working beautifully yesterday, but tomorrow might require a whole new approach. Look at the Israelites for example: in the desert they didn't have to prepare for certain challenges; all they had to do was trust God to meet their basic needs for food and clothing. God defeated their enemies, and showered down bread from heaven and water from a rock; He also placed an anointing on their clothes in order to make them impervious to the wear and tear of time. But when it came time to enter into the Promised Land, the Israelites had to learn how to fight, and they had to learn how to grow their own food and find their own water; they had to develop an entirely different set of skills in order to survive in the Promised Land. In fact, God stopped sending the manner from heaven the moment they ate the produce from the Land of Canaan (Joshua 5:12). The anointing that preserved the Israelites' clothing lifted the moment they crossed over the Jordan River and into the Land of Canaan. Some anointings and blessings were meant only for a certain season; and now that *that* season has passed, it is now time for a fresh anointing, a new strategy, and a new skill set. People change with new seasons. Attitudes change with new seasons. The Apostle Paul was raised as a Pharisee before coming to Christ. As a Pharisee, he was taught to view women negatively. He was taught to look down upon Gentiles and women. This view was in stark contrast to the view of women by Jesus, who even allowed women to travel with He and His disciples (technically, you can say Jesus had women disciples. No traditional Jewish rabbi allowed women accompany them in their ministry. Jesus, however, shattered traditional roles imposed on women and allowed them to travel as well as minister with Him) (Luke 8:1-3). Eventually, Paul had to shake certain attitudes if he was to prosper in ministry. God challenged him to do so by placing the key to his ministry's breakthrough in the hands of a woman. For Acts 16:14 reveals to us that while Paul was preaching, God caused a woman named Lydia to take notice of him—Lydia was a multi-millionaire who was well capable of financing Paul's ministry, which was what Paul needed. Notice that the financial breakthrough for Paul came from a person that Paul, had he not been converted and released his prejudices towards women, would have shunned. Some Christians' prejudices are preventing them from accepting the people God is trying to connect them with in order to accomplish His will. The people we expect to come through for us tend not to, but the very people we swear we'd never get tied-up with end-up being the ones God uses to get us to where we belong. God is unpredictable. God is predictably unpredictable. The only thing from God we can expect with certainty is that He will move in unexpected ways in our lives, but we must be willing to shift, to change, to move with Him as He moves; we must be willing to abandon our carnal thinking and be conformed to God's Word—in Christ, the world's thinking and understanding doesn't apply. The racial and political identities we take on don't apply in Christ. For Galatians 3:26-28 declares,

> "For you are all children of God through faith
> in Christ Jesus. And all who have been unit-

ed with Christ in baptism have put on Christ,
like putting on new clothes. There is no longer Jew or Gentile, slave or free, male and female. For you are all one in Christ Jesus."

We must see ourselves and others through the lens
of the Bible, not society. This is what prepares us
for the next level living, the next level blessings, the
next level anointing God has for us. We can't predict
God, but we can prepare for Him; and we do so by
allowing our minds to be transformed by His Word.
God moves in the lives of those who are ready and
willing to go to the next level, not those who want to
remain trapped in their old ways.

Paul, in 2 Timothy 2:15, told us to "study to
show thyself approved unto God," letting God know
that we're ready to work for Him. The indication that
we're ready to handle what God has for us is that we
are spiritually mature in the understanding of God's
Word, "rightly dividing" (*orthotomeō* in the Greek,
meaning "to make straight and smooth, to handle
aright, to teach the truth directly and correctly") the
word of truth. Elevation comes with revelation, and
revelation comes through studying the Word so that
we can understand God, His ways, and His will. The
Israelites didn't want to change their way of thinking in the desert, and for this reason God refused to
let them journey into the next level of their lives. Instead, God let that hard-hearted, stiff-necked, older
generation die in the wilderness. Be careful that you

don't allow experience to stiffen you and cause you to believe you have a patten on success. Don't think that the way you've done things in the past is going to work always. God may be calling for a change in strategy, and pride and a closed-mind will cause you to miss what God is doing now.

NEW PLACES, NEW DISCOVERIES

I didn't realize that I could write until I hung up the gloves. My goal was the boxing ring, not the pulpit or the literary world. When God took my life in the direction He wanted it to go, I was unhappy. I didn't want to preach. I didn't want to go into the ministry. And then, when I did enter the ministry, I thought that this would be all: I would stand behind a podium and talk with a Bible in my hand. I didn't know that God would later place book-writing and publishing in my heart. I didn't know I would end-up becoming an entrepreneur. I never imagined I would even end-up writing and producing plays, doing graphic arts, ghostwriting for other authors, promoting Holy Hip Hop concerts, putting together events outside of the church, winning several poetry competitions on an international level (earning me tens of thousands of dollars in cash), and doing all of the other things I've done. The pulpit is just one of several things God placed in my heart. When God snatches you away from your dream and dumps you in a position you didn't expect to be in, it is because He is getting ready to open you up and bring more out of you than you realize is inside of you; God is getting ready to take you places that you could only imagine. God is trying to create multiple streams of blessings in your life, not just that one stream (that job, that career) you *narrow-mindedly* envisioned for yourself. God is a God of plenty. He promised to do "infinitely more than we might ask or think" (Ephesians 3:20, NLT). Hear that? Infinitely more! But His blessings always start out small: with a seed, with a small situation, with a challenge we don't expect, or with an act of obedience we probably don't think will do much for us up the road. Don't despise small beginnings (Zechariah 4:10). Don't underestimate situations that look like they won't lead you anywhere. Don't assume that because you're not where you expected to be that you're cursed (1 Peter 4:12). When God is with you He gives you His peace and assurance even in the midst of storms, but He's also teaching you how to follow and obey Him in the small things, and to stop waiting on big opportunities to perform and start doing the little things He commands you to do now.

I can recall one night when God taught me a valuable lesson concerning not underestimating situations because of how things look. I was teaching a Friday Night Bible Study at the time. Only a handful of people would show up—fifteen, maybe twenty. At the end of service I'd take up an offering. At the most, I would get $25, maybe $30 or $40. But this one particular Friday night only one person showed up for service. I was a little frustrated, but the Holy Spirit told me to press on anyway and teach as if the room was running over. I taught a full message with passion, not allowing the scene of empty chairs to deter me. Afterwards, the lady who was there, without speaking a word or giving any indication that the message blessed her, proceeded out of the door. As she was leaving, she placed a check face-down on the table where I was seated (where I taught from). After she left, I picked up the check. I didn't expect it to be much, but I was blown away when noticing that it was made out in the amount of $500. Ironically, I received my biggest offering from my smallest audience. Never let what you see deter you from obeying God. You never know how God is going to move in your life. Big blessings can—and often do—come in small packages...when you follow Christ.

In 1 Kings chapter 17, the prophet Elijah had to learn how to follow God. During a tough drought God led Elijah from one location to another and fed him through the most unlikely of hosts: ravens. Ravens are programmed to feed on dead things, not feed living things; but God reprogrammed the ravens to feed Elijah...as long as Elijah was where God placed him. There was a brook where God put him; things were looking good at the moment; but then, when it was time to move, God let the brook dry up and the ravens stop coming—the anointing for the brook and the ravens lifted, and God was now leading Elijah to a new location. God had already gone ahead of Elijah and docked at a widow's house, which is where God instructed Elijah to go to next. Elijah went to the widow's house. She was preparing food for she and her son with the last little bit of the supplies that were left. After eating this meal, they were prepared to face starvation and death, but God had a plan to bless both Elijah and the widow woman and her son. As she obeyed the prophet, who instructed her to feed him first, God restored her food supply, causing it to overflow; but this blessing came as a result of one small act of obedience: bake the preacher a biscuit. God placed an anointing on her food that out-lasted the drought (vs. 14); but once the rain started falling again, it was time for a new strategy—that anointing on her storehouse was going to expire. It's time to seek God for the next step. You can't survive off of yesterday's anointing.

THE GOD OF MULTIPLE STONES

Solomon wrote in Ecclesiastes 11:1-2,

> "Send your grain across the seas, and in time, profits will flow back to you. But divide your investments among many places, for you do not know what risks might lie ahead" (NLT).

Like I stated earlier, I don't know if David was expecting Goliath's friends to show up that day in the valley or if David was simply preparing to have some back-up stones just in case the first one missed; but in either case, he demonstrated a divine principle: let God open-up multiple streams of blessings in your life. Never limit yourself to just one stone (stream). God prepares us ahead of time for the unexpected. You don't know if, or even when, that job is going to shut-down, that company is going to close, or you'll be fired; so, don't limit yourself to just that one job. Let God guide you into several ventures that will provide increase in your life. Let God reveal to you other talents and gifts you have. Let God speak to you about other things other than that which you're completely focused on. Let God expand your vision so that it is bigger than a 9 to 5. You are more than a 9 to 5 (job). Don't despise a 9 to 5. Thank God for a source of income, but let Him lead you in a strategy to bring greater increase to your house. Take some of that 9 to 5 money and use it for investments that will set you up for a brighter financial future. Don't be like the "unprofitable servant" in Matthew chapter twenty-five who buried his money in the ground as opposed to investing it. He thought that by simply *saving* money in an account he would secure his master's money, but he was surprised by his master's reaction to his decision, which was a harsh reaction.

In Malachi chapter three, God asks for a tithe (a tenth of one's income). God's promise to the Israelites was that He would bless them with a harvest that would not be destroyed by insects nor cast its yield before time and be useless. Through obedience the heavens (1st heaven, referring to the sky) would be opened to the people and rain would be provided for the seeds they sowed. God would transform seeds into fruit trees; He would produce much fruit from one little seed; He would produce much from only a little. One seed produces much fruit containing many seeds. God is a God of multiplication. He can take the little from your job and multiply it, but you must trust Him and give Him the little He asks for. The tithe is not for God's benefit, it's for you benefit; it is the act of sacrifice that procures the favor of God on the rest of your finances. He wants to use the 10% to bless His church and then lead you concerning the 90%, showing you where to invest it so that you can have more streams available just in case that 9 to 5 dries up . . . which it eventually will. God speaks to us about reaping and sowing in 1 Corinthians chapter 9. When we sow seed into God's Kingdom (ministry), He causes His favor to abound in our direction. God is trying to give you wisdom. Proverbs 8:12 says, "I wisdom dwell with prudence, and find out knowledge of witty inventions." God is trying to get ideas to you that can bring increase into your life, but you have to seek His face and gain His wisdom, not the world's wisdom (James 3:14-17). God is trying to speak to you today. He wants to put you in a blessed position today. Follow His plan today. If you choose not to or choose to delay your obedience, you do so at your own peril.

We serve a God of multiple stones. He's an unpredictable God preparing us for the unpredictable. There's one thing we can predict, however, and it is this: everything God does in our lives when we surrender to Him is to bless us, prosper us, and give us a glorious ending (Jeremiah 29:11).

CHAPTER 8 OBJECTIVES:

•Take time to invest in yourself by finding out what talents and abilities God has given you in life. Find out what makes you different and significant; what problem(s) are you most equipped to solve in life. To do this, you will need to ask God to guide you. He placed the treasure in you; therefore, He knows what's inside of you better than anyone. Pray, "Lord, I thank You that You have given me talents, gifts and abilities. Lord, I pray that You will reveal to me the things You have given me to make an impact in this world and in the lives of others, and use these things for Your Kingdom sake so that You may be glorified in the earth."

•Cast off labels placed on you by the world: stupid, slow, dumb, incorrigible, useless, unable to change, defeated, useless, inferior, etc. Begin to speak what God's Word says about you today. Remember: As a man thinketh, so is he (Proverbs 23:7).

•Ask God to guide you into discovering at least 7 different streams of income. Develop one stream and master it, then develop and master the next.

•Practice being a giver. Begin tithing if you aren't doing so already. Also, sow seeds offerings into the lives of others, especially anointed vessels of God.

•Practice being a good steward over the finances God gives you. Don't be an impulsive spender, or a wasteful person. Be wise with the resources God has given you. Pray for wisdom in this matter.

FINAL WORD

LIFE IS NEVER EASY FOR A KING in the making. Misunderstandings, disappointments, rejections, loneliness, ostracization, frustrations, and discouragement is a part of the process of becoming a king. There is something supernatural underpinning this process. There is something supernatural at play in the life of a king—in your life. Can you feel it? Can you sense it? Can you sense that there's something bubbling up on the inside of you that has to come out, something God has placed inside of your being; and that there are forces desperately trying to conceal that which is on the inside of you, that which God has purposed for you to walk in? Do you think it is a mere coincidence that your life was marred by so much pain, that you've had so many challenges, and that you've experienced so many set-backs and let-downs? Could you feel the real you being suppressed with each hurt; your essence being buried beneath each layer of false identity being imposed on you by others or even yourself, covering up the person God intended for you to be? Do you think it is a coincidence that you have arrived at the place where everyone, including your own family, has written you off? Kings are forged under such conditions. Unfortunately, the path to greatness is paved with the gravel of pain and hardship. This is because the responsibility that comes along with greatness is mighty. If you can but fight through these things and ascend to throne of dominance over your own thoughts and emotions; if you could perceive life through God's eyes rather than through the lens of carnal understanding, then you will discover that you are not what others have declared you to be. You were designed to be what God declared you to be. The biggest giants are the ones in our heads, sitting right between our ears. It's there where the greatest battle lies. The tendency to view ourselves as grasshoppers in the face of seemingly insurmountable, unconquerable odds is the greater issue. Your problem may be big, it may be menacing, but it's not big enough to intimidate the God who created heaven and earth (God Jehovah). In the eyes of God, the challenges staring you in your face are just blips, small dots, specks of dust. When you cast off the lie that claims you're just a grasshopper, and you realize that you're more than a conqueror *only* through Christ Jesus; when you slay the lie that God doesn't love you, that you deserve to be trampled on, that you're insignificant, and that you were meant to die in the condition that you are in and you accept the fact that you were designed and equipped by God to conquer your giants, that's when you will realize that your lack of size isn't a disadvantage, but rather, it's an opportunity to prove the enormity of the size of the God operating inside of you. Faith births kings inside of us; adversity brings the king out of us.

PRAYER

Dear Heavenly Father, I thank You for Your grace and Your mercy. I thank You that You called me to be an overcomer. You called me to be more than a conquerer in Your Word. I thank You that You have endowed me with everything I need to fulfill Your will. You created me with treasure already buried on the inside of me. Open me up and bring out that treasure. Lead and guide me in Your perfect will. It's not about me and what I want; it's about You and what You have purposed for my life. Lead me to my place of dominion in life, which is the place You have predestined for me to be in. I know the enemy will try to hinder me from getting there, and will even send attacks my way while there; but I am committed to doing Your will and not backing down. I know that no weapon formed against me shall prosper, and that every giant that rises against me will fall as I do Your will.

Father, cleanse my heart and mind. If I have any prejudices, strongholds, bitterness and animosity, un-forgiveness, misconceptions, or wrong perceptions of You as well as myself, take them out of me. Give me a clean heart and the right spirit. Free me from the chains of yesterday so that I may move forward into the purpose You have for me.

Restore unto me the joy, zest, zeal, passion, fire, capacity to dream, and confidence the enemy stole from me. I release the trauma of every past incident that derailed me from the path you placed me on. I am free! I am a new person in Christ Jesus! My past is simply my testimony, and not my prison. Transform my thinking with Your Word. Give me wisdom to do Your will. Let me enter into an intimate walk with You. Let me come to know Your power and presence. Teach me how to hear and recognize Your voice, Holy Spirit. Teach me how to rest confidently in Your power and might. For it's not by power or might, as You have declared in Your Word; but it's by Your Holy Spirit that Your will is accomplished in my life. You are my source and my strength. I repent for placing my confidence in the flesh, and for placing my hope in the strong arm of the flesh (people; carnal thinking; the world), which you said would fail me in your Word. I denounce any and all ties to the occult, to witchcraft and sorcery, and to the Kingdom of Satan, and I surrender totally to Your authority and will. I denounce selfishness, and the love of the world, and cast down the wall of pride that causes me to be hard-hearted towards You. I denounce iniquity. I repent of all sins I've committed against You, and I choose to live for You and You alone. I love You and thank You. It's in Jesus name I pray, Amen.

OTHER BOOKS BY T&J PUBLISHERS

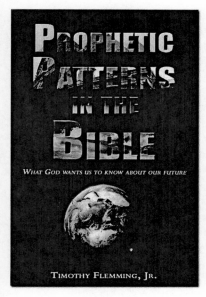

Published in 2010, this is the debut book by Timothy Flemming, Jr. This book reveals the patterns that are found in the Bible: patterns concerning the rise and fall of nations, of prophetic events, and patterns God uses as it pertains to releasing His blessings and judgment in the earth. The foundational scripture is found in Ecclesiastes 1:9 which says, "The thing that hath been, it is that which shall be; and that which is done is that which shall be done: and there is no new thing under the sun."

Available on Amazon.com and Barnes&Noble.com
$14.99   156 pgs.

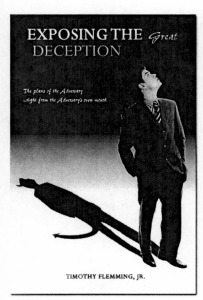

Published in 2012, this is the explosive follow-up book to Prophetic Patterns in the Bible. This book goes into greater deal concerning prophetic events, bringing to light revelations concerning the rise of the antichrist, the nature of the antichrist, the many counterfeit messiahs Jesus said would arrive before His coming, the rise of occultism in society, and the creation of the New World Order that is prophesied to come before Christ makes His final return.

Available on Amazon.com and Barnes&Noble.com
$21.95   500 pgs.

OTHER BOOKS BY T&J PUBLISHERS

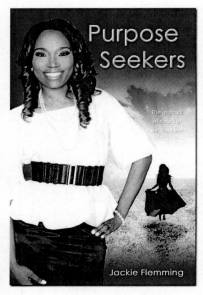

Published in 2014, this is the debut book by Jackie Flemming. This life-changing and incredible book follows the events of Jackie's life, revealing how she went from a life of promiscuity, drugs and rebelliousness to a life of purity, godliness and true happiness. It covers topics such as: hearing the voice of the Holy Spirit; deliverance from soul-ties; discovering your identity in Christ; and more. Each chapter ends with a prayer of impartation and contains faith building exercises. This is a must have! Go to **www.LadyJackie.com**

Available on Amazon.com and Barnes&Noble.com
$14.95   133 pgs.

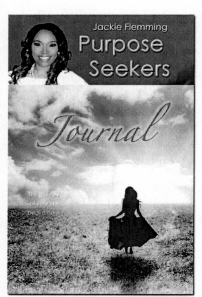

Published in 2014, this is the journal companion to the book *Purpose Seeker*, written by Jackie Flemming. This journal is filled with faith building exercises and valuable revelations on finding your God-given purpose that are not found in the main book. This is an excellent resource to have. Go to **www.LadyJackie.com**

Available on Amazon.com and Barnes&Noble.com
$10.95   90 pgs.

ABOUT THE AUTHOR

Timothy Flemming, Jr. is an author, entrepreneur, public speaker, playwrite, poet, and minister of the Gospel. He is the founder of T&J Publishers and the author of several books, including *Prophetic Patterns in the Bible* and *Exposing the Great Deception*. He has won several awards for poetry. Timothy is also a husband and father of three. For more information, go to:

www.TandJPublishers.com
www.TimothyFlemmingJr.com

CPSIA information can be obtained
at www.ICGtesting.com
Printed in the USA
FFOW01n0432211115
18795FF